BATHROOM

ALBERTA
HISTORY

Intriguing and Entertaining Facts
about our Province's Past

Marina Michaelides

BLUE
BIKE
BOOKS

The Publisher: Blue Bike Books

Library and Archives Canada Cataloguing in Publication

Michaelides, Marina, 1963–
   Bathroom book of Alberta history : intriguing and entertaining facts about our province's past / Marina Michaelides ; Roger Garcia, Graham Johnson, illustrators

   (Bathroom books of Canada ; 10)

   ISBN-13: 978-1-897278-17-8
   ISBN-10: 1-897278-17-9

   1. Alberta—History—Miscellanea. I. Garcia, Roger, 1976–
II. Title. III. Series.

FC3661.M529 2006   971.23   C2006-904131-8

Project Director: Nicholle Carrière
Project Editor: Tom Monto
Illustrations: Roger Garcia, Graham Johnson
Cover Image: Roger Garcia

We acknowledge the support of the Alberta Foundation for the Arts for our publishing program.

PC: P5

DEDICATION

To my darling Anna.
Who loved so deeply,
laughed so heartily,
shone so sweetly,
just not for very long.
Now she soars, as one again.

CONTENTS

INTRODUCTION 6

THE FIRST ALBERTANS
Dinosaurs and Sponges. 8
Early "Man" and First Nations. 9

THE WHITE MAN COMETH
HBC and the Fur Trade 13
Rupert's Land Becomes the NWT 16
David Thompson: Canada's Surveyor 18
Alberta Places Get Names 19

FUR TRADERS AND MISSIONARIES
Henday Sees Alberta and Leaves. 22
The Fur Trade Makes the Natives Giddy 23
Mackenzie Travels the North 24
Missionaries Follow in HBC Footsteps 27

THE WHISKEY WARS AND COPS ON HORSEBACK
U.S. Whiskey Posts Trade in Violence 30
Go West, Young (NWMP) Men 32
The Blackfoot Meet the Greenhorns 34

FIRST NATIONS AND COWBOYS
The Queen and Her Wards 35
Good Grass Brings John Ware to Alberta 37
Calgary Stampede: Some Excitement 40
Pat Burns: A Meatpacker from Way Back 42

HOMESTEADS, RAILWAYS AND MODERN FARMERS
The Seeds of Alberta Agriculture 43
The Calgary–Edmonton Corridor: A Dense Place to Live. 44

KLONDIKE DAYS
Gold Rushes and Lost Mines 64

PROVINCIAL BIRTH
Province of Alberta Blossoms 67

EDUCATION
The Days of Chalk and Slateboards 71
Some Things Stay the Same 72

LAW AND ORDER
What Goes Around Comes Around 75

PROHIBITION AND OTHER COCKTAILS
Liquor and the Law 78

TWO WORLD WARS
World War I 80
Between the Wars 81
World War II 82

SPORTS
Ice and Snow 86
Albertans with Balls 89
Reaching High 91
Horsing Around 92
Winning at Games 93

PROVINCE BURNS BRIGHT
Energetic Alberta 96

CULTURE
Musical Milestones 103
Stage and Screen 107
The Printed Word 111
Radio and Television 114
Alberta's Arts Advantage 116

SCIENCE AND INVENTIONS
From Bridges to Bio-Tech 119

POLITICS
Women Get Involved 123
Strange Bedfellows 125

MEDICAL AND HEALTH
Getting Better 132

CULINARY DELIGHTS AND DISASTERS
Growing Success 135
Cattle and Confectionery 136

THE BEST IN THE BUSINESS
Early Success 139
Exceptional Albertans 140

GEOGRAPHY AND THE ENVIRONMENT
Natural History 143

ODDS, ENDS AND SOME SURPRISES
Firsts and Lasts 150
Highs and Lows 156
Strange But True 163

INTRODUCTION

Modern Alberta is the product of invaders. I'm one of them, one of millions of new Canadians who chose to make this province home. So, it's a privilege to have had the time in writing this book, to plunder the province's history in search of humorous nuggets, matters of fact, surprises, celebrations, first, lasts and mistakes, to tell the tale of Alberta's roots and how Alberta has evolved into one of the most prosperous places on earth. For now. Just like the weather, good times and bad in Alberta appear in cycles—near-cosmic ups and hellishly difficult downs.

The Province's contemporary history is relatively short but as rich as the veins of oil lying beneath its surface. Since Anthony Henday's arrival in 1754, immigrants from all over the world have arrived and taken over the land from the First Nations, to trade, ranch, homestead, farm and prospect for gold, oil, gas, coal and lumber. This book is a quick and quirky overview of those dreams and achievements, peppered with the bizarre and outrageous.

History isn't just about survival in a harsh environment and conquering Nature. It's about how we enjoy being human. I found much to celebrate in the cultural traditions Alberta's settlers brought with them. And the new ones emerging amid an ethnic mosaic of peoples within a vast land of wilderness, forests, mountains, lakes and stunning natural beauty.

Snippets and snapshots, included in this book, hopefully will cause us to wonder at Albertans' scientific ingenuity and artistic creativity, medical marvels and inspirational leaders, and champions of champions. As counterpoint, there are also the no-good specimens of the human race that don't deserve more time than it takes to shake a head in disbelief.

When I first arrived in Alberta and wandered through its ravines and rivers, the pioneering spirit of this province was never far away. I wondered how on earth people made it through savage winters and dustbowl summers. Despite the sophistication of this province's ballets, industries and shopping malls, Alberta is a product of its landscape, a place where nature is awesome, a reminder to every Albertan and visitor to celebrate our good fortune and to leave behind a legacy to those who follow in our footsteps. This book is a celebration of all that.

DINOSAURS AND SPONGES

Rock Dwellers

Invertebrate sea creatures living in a shallow sea covering the whole of Western Canada, are the first known inhabitants of the region now known as Alberta. Their fossils are immortalized in the Burgess Shale, located on the west side of the BC-Alberta border in Yoho National Park. No examples are visible on the Alberta side.

Roots of Alberta's Wealth
The sponges, coral and other sea inhabitants die, and their bodies turn into the oil upon which Alberta's economy of today is built.

Stuck in the Middle
Around 440 million years ago, Alberta and British Columbia straddle the equator.

Oldest Land Inhabitants
Dinosaurs roam the land for 160 million years and become extinct about 65 million years ago. Alberta's own dinosaur, the Albertosaurus, is a look-alike cousin of the T-rex.

Egg-stinct
The first dinosaur eggs are discovered in May 1877 when Wendy Sloboda spots the little darlings in Devil's Coulee, near Warner in southern Alberta.

EARLY "MAN" AND FIRST NATIONS

The Bering Bridge

About 30,000 years ago, the first humanoid "Albertans" cross over from Siberia on a land bridge now covered by the Bering Sea.

First Signs

An 11,000-year-old bison skull with a primitive hammer embedded in it is discovered on the banks of the Oldman River, near Taber in the late 1950s. It's the first scientifically undisputed evidence of man's existence in the region.

Old Argument

But, a child's skull, discovered in Taber in 1961, still has scientists arguing. Some have dated it at 30,000 years, while others claim it's closer to 60,000 BC. Either way, the bones are the oldest human remains in North America.

Blackfoot Boulders

A chain of 2000 massive boulders, called erratics, lie between present-day Rocky Mountain House and the U.S. border. They are thought to have been transported there within massive glaciers originating in Jasper. "Okotok" is the Blackfoot word for rock. The largest erratic in the world, Big Rock, sits 20 kilometres west of the town of Okotoks.

Preserved Status

In 1978, Big Rock, which is 9 metres high and 41 metres long and weighs more than 16,000 tonnes, becomes the first natural feature in Alberta to become an official provincial historic site.

Too Hot to Handle

About 8000 years ago, the prairies turn into scorching deserts.

Cooling-Off Period

About 4500 years ago, forests grow back and hunting nomadic hunters move in. Families of primitive pedestrians populate the land for the next few thousand years.

Buffalo Jumps

For centuries, the First Nation's livelihood depends on bison, which roam the plains in numbers estimated at 60 million. An effective way to kill hundreds at a time is to chase the beasts over a precipice and then carve up the carcasses in the camp below—something Prairie inhabitants have been doing for over 6000 years.

Bison Bits

The beast's flesh is food, its hide clothing and tipi covers, its bones tools, its dung fuel. "Shaganappi" is the name given to tendons and strips of rawhide. After shrinking and hardening by drying, they can be used as cord or twine. In the late 1800s, hundreds of tonnes of bison bones are sent East by rail to be ground up and used as fertilizer.

Head-Smashed-In

One of the world's oldest, largest and best-preserved buffalo jumps is Head-Smashed-In Buffalo Jump, 18 kilometres northwest of Fort Macleod. The site is named after a brave who got too close to the action and got squashed. Head-Smashed-In is designated a UNESCO World Heritage Site in 1981, joining the ranks of global treasures that include the Egyptian pyramids, Stonehenge and the Galapagos Islands. The Duke and Duchess of York officially open the site to the public on July 23, 1987.

Potty on the Plains
The oldest pottery fragments found in Alberta are thought to be around 2000 years old.

Tools of the Trade

About 600 AD, the bow and arrow are first used by aboriginals in Alberta. About this time, families create small groups (bands) that hunt together.

Sacred Skeletons

Bison are revered in "ribstones"—boulders with grooves pecked out to represent the bison skeleton—scattered across the prairies. Superb examples of 1000-year-old ribstones can be seen in the village of Viking, in central Alberta.

BWM

Before the white man arrives, the First Nations people live in small bands with their own languages and culture in the province's different geographical areas.

Forest Firsts

The forests north of the North Saskatchewan River are home to the Athabascan people—the tribes called Beaver, Chipewyan, Slaves and Sekani.

Cree Central

The Cree, migrating westward, settle in the central plains.

Saskatchewan Divide

The Blackfoot and Sarcee roam the prairies south of the North Saskatchewan River, while the Bloods and the Gros Ventre (French for "big bellies"!) cover the southeastern prairies.

Other First Nations

The Kootenay and Stony tribes live in the foothills south of Banff. Southwest Alberta is home to the Shoshoni tribe and the Piegan.

DID YOU  KNOW?

The phrase "dog days" comes from the days when Blackfoot use dogs for transport. Better transport means more food can be carried and people can spend less time hunting.

HBC AND THE FUR TRADE

A New Country

In 1670, Charles II of England sells Rupert's Land, the territory from Ontario to BC, to the Hudson's Bay Company (HBC), and at the same time, also grants the company exclusive trading rights in the region.

Cree Wholesalers

Around 1700, the Cree begin to flood in from the east, bringing with them the spoils of savvy trading with the white men. They sell beaver, bison and any other pelt they can catch or buy from other tribes to the European fur traders, in exchange for tools and guns. The Cree soon dominate the prairies, pushing the Chipewyan tribes north and east of the Athabasca region.

Hunter Horsemen

Life on the plains changes around 1730 with the arrival of horses originally exported to Mexico from Spain. Using this method of transport, the Blackfoot and Piegans began to carry heavy tipis and surplus food longer distances than previously possible. With this new "technology," the Blackfoot and Piegans become quite numerous.

Right Royal Hands Off!!!

George III, the king of England, issues a Royal Proclamation in 1763 that First Nations should not be disturbed in their use and enjoyment of the land.

Bountiful Bison

In 1830, around 40 million bison still roamed the plains. It took 70 more years to wipe them off the face of North America's map.

Blackfoot Comeback

The Blackfoot, ruthless, fierce and brave, fight against the Cree and steal some of their guns. By 1865, armed now with weapons *and* horse transport, the Blackfoot conquer the plains and control them until around 1900. They hunt in large groups and fill up their larders, which they can now carry with them.

Alberta's First Vehicle

Red River carts appear on the prairies in the 1850s. They are made entirely of wood with a tapered tree trunk for an axle and wheels made of solid wood, covered with rawhide to soften the ride.

Screeched to Death
The wooden limbs of the cart scrape so badly on the bone-dry axle. They make a horrendous screech so obnoxious the Métis claim the noise is responsible for driving the bison off the plains for good.

Carrying Carrion
By 1850, convoys of up to 1500 Red River carts are used to transport meat culled in massive Métis bison hunts. The hunts produce over half a million kilograms of buffalo meat in one go.

First Festivals
The First Nations know how to party. Whole tribes gather for weeklong feasts and dancing. In what is called the "Sun Dance," braves prove their courage and strength in endurance rituals and attain status as warriors.

Natural Medicine
The Blackfoot are deeply religious and worship the sun, moon, stars and the powers of animals, from which they derive their "medicine."

Wiped Out
But the First Nations have no immunity to white man's diseases, including smallpox. The first plague in 1781 wipes out half the plains people. Another in 1837 wipes out two-thirds of the Blackfoot. In 1870, a third epidemic reaches its peak and almost wipes out the Blackfoot entirely.

The Dead of Winter
A winter epidemic of scarlet fever in 1864 kills an estimated 1100 of the Niitsi-tapi tribe across Alberta.

Land Trades
In 1867, the Dominion of Canada is born when Québec, Ontario, New Brunswick and Nova Scotia join Confederation. The rest of the country, known as Rupert's Land, has little organized government.

RUPERT'S LAND BECOMES THE NWT

Buy Back

In 1869, the HBC sells Rupert's Land and the North-West Territories back to the British Crown for £300,000, which in turn transfers the land to the new Dominion of Canada.

Independence Movement
The Red River Rebellion of 1869, led by Métis Louis Riel, explodes in Manitoba in an attempt to secure the region of the Red River as a province under Métis control. The revolt is triggered by the imminent arrival of the CPR's "iron horse" and the granting of traditional hunting lands to build the railway. Soldiers sent to quell the rebellion take three months on horseback to get to the battlefields. In 1885, during the second Riel Rebellion, soldiers from Toronto reach Saskatoon by train in less than a week.

Guarding a Safe Passage

Fort Normandeau is built as an NWMP outpost during the 1885 Riel Rebellion. The purpose is to protect the Red Deer river crossing, the safest place to cross the river and long-used by the Natives as the gateway between north and south Alberta. A "stopping house" (hostel) is built there in 1884. The 1885 fort is under the command of Lt. Normandeau for whom the new citadel is named.

Dividing Line
The 49th parallel is surveyed in 1872 and demarcates the U.S.'s northern border with Canada.

The First Soup Kitchen
Most of the bison are gone, and the NWMP must feed 7000 starving Natives during the winter of 1879.

Town Inc.
In 1891, the population of Calgary is nearly 4000. When the city incorporates in 1894, it is the only community between the West Coast and Winnipeg that has a water works and sewage system.

City. Inc.
Edmonton incorporates as a town in 1892 with a population of 700. When it incorporates as a city in 1904 its population has reached 8350.

Second Wipe Out
By the end of the 1800s, bison are on the verge of extinction north of the 49th parallel. Their virtual disappearance means the end of the First Nations' way of life.

Bison Back From the Dead

Only 100 or so bison survive as farmyard pets. A herd of wild bison are discovered in Banff National Park in 1912, a big surprise because it was thought there were no more to be found. The herd is sent to Northern Alberta for safekeeping where they breed successfully to populate Wood Buffalo National Park.

Keeping Beauty and the Beast Safe...
Wood Buffalo National Park is designated a UNESCO World Heritage Site in 1983, Canada's largest national park. With an area of more than 44,000 km², the park is the size of Denmark and lies on Alberta's northern border partly in the Northwest Territories.

...and Sound
Wood Buffalo Park's boreal forests and plains make up some of the largest undisturbed grass-and-sedge meadows left in North America which in turn sustain the largest free-roaming herd of bison in the world.

DAVID THOMPSON: CANADA'S SURVEYOR

The First Surveyor

In 1807, Welsh-born David Thompson becomes the first white man to discover a gateway through the Rockies, at Athabasca Pass. He travels to the Pacific Ocean via the Columbia River. He is also Canada's most important surveyor, charting almost 13 million km^2 of northwest Canada, using a sextant and the stars. Aboriginals affectionately nickname him "Koo Koo Sint" ("Star Gazer").

Spot On
Thompson's 1814 map is so accurate, it is the basis for many of the maps issued by the Canadian government and the railways 100 years later.

A Moral Responsibility

Unlike other explorers of the time, Thompson refuses to trade alcohol for furs. Thompson's employer, The North West Company, forces him to take trading alcohol with him on his trips. Thompson again and again reports to his superiors that "accidents" befell his whiskey-laden horses, that they "slipped" or "slid" off cliff edges, taking the booze with them.

Fair Game
Thompson takes a First Nations wife, Charlotte Small, and does not abandon his "country wife," as many other fur traders do once the work is done. Thompson lived with her until his death. Together they had 13 children.

Posthumous Thanks
Thompson dies destitute and in near obscurity in 1857. A century later he is honoured on a 1957 postage stamp.

ALBERTA PLACES GET NAMES

Pinch Me, Is That True?

When a 1868 prospecting expedition led by W.S. Lees and Joe Healy lose their pliers in a southern Alberta river, the story gives the town of "Pincher Creek" its name.

Canada's Most Famous Rock Star

Joseph Tyrrell (1858–1957), a geologist and cartographer, discovers coal in the south of the province in 1884. As he canoes down the Red Deer River valley on June 9 that year, he made his greatest find—a 70-million-year-old skull of an Albertosaurus and one of the world's largest dinosaur-rich deposits. The "Alberta Lizard," or Albertosaurus, measures 9 metres long and looks like a T-rex.

Expensive Rocks

In later life, Tyrell becomes a mining consultant in the Klondike and later a millionaire owner/manager of gold mines at Kirkland Lake, Ontario.

No Canuck Diggers

Tyrell wasn't a paleontologist and there were no other Canadians at the time with these skills, so most of Alberta's remaining dinosaur discoveries are made by Americans. Barnum Brown, a Kansas-born dinosaur hunter, finds and removes 16 skeletons between 1909 and 1914 and ships them to the American Museum of Natural History in New York City, where they remain today.

Protection Long Time Coming

It isn't until 1978 that fossils become a protected species under a federal Historical Resources Act, and only in the year 2000 does the Alberta government make it illegal to export dinosaur bones and fossils outside the province.

Painter of People

Irish Canadian Paul Kane explores people. He is one of Canada's most important painters of Aboriginals, his work considered part of the nation's heritage. In 1846, he spends a year in the Edmonton area and near Fort Carlton in west central Saskatchewan, sketching people of the tribes. From these he produces over 100 paintings.

Delicacies on Demand
For Christmas dinner at Fort Edmonton, Kane is served boiled bison hump, a boiled bison calf, and mouffle—dried moose nose.

People on the Prairies

John Palliser, an Irish-born Canadian, is sent by the British Government on an expedition in 1857 to explore the uncharted territory of the prairies south of Edmonton, north of Lethbridge and west of Winnipeg. His mission is to determine the feasibility of homesteading in the area.

Dry Premonition

Palliser says no. In his opinion the area is too arid and lacks stable vegetation to sustain agriculture. The British Parliament follows his advice and homesteading on the prairies waits another three decades. His assessment proves tragically correct in the 1930s drought, a spell of devastating winds and heat that wipes out 10,000 farms.

An Honourable Legacy

The bar at the five-star Palliser Hotel, Calgary is ironically a favourite businessmen's watering hole in that city today. In 1929, Winston Churchill attends a luncheon at the hotel, in Palliser's honour.

Not What He Seems
Curiously, Palliser is also rumoured to be a spy, working for Confederate states in the U.S. and for Caribbean governments.

Gentlemen Hunters

The Rockies' first "tourist" is the Earl of Southesk. He blazes a trail for British gentlemen on hunting expeditions who, like him, seem to think Western Canada is their own personal playground. On his 1859 visit, the Earl brings along a portable rubber bathtub so he can wash in the style to which he has become accustomed.

The Champagne Safari

In 1934, independently wealthy Charles Bedaux spends one quarter of a million dollars in a 2400-kilometre adventure from Edmonton through the Canadian Rockies to Alaska. He took with him his wife, his mistress, 53 cowboys, 130 horses and five specially made half-track tractors loaded with twenty tonnes of equipment luxuries such as truffles, Devonshire cream, French wine, silver cutlery, liver paté, caviar and several trunks worth of silk pyjamas and ladies shoes. Part of today's Alaska Highway follows the Bedaux route.

White at the Top
The year 1873 goes down in history as the date that the first white men, Michael Phillipps and John Collins, reach the top of the Crowsnest Pass.

HENDAY SEES ALBERTA AND LEAVES

Black Meets White

Sent by the Hudson Bay Company to trade Blackfoot furs, Anthony Henday becomes the first white man to step on present-day Alberta soil in 1754, at the place where the village of Chauvin stands today.

First Powwow

Henday is the guest of honour at the West's first "trade conference," the first time many Alberta First Nations meet a white man. 2000 curious Blackfoot set up a massive camp of 200 tents laid out in two neat rows, the chief's tent at the end. They lay on a great feast but don't want to trade.

A Very Long Journey

Henday's journey begins at York Factory in Hudson Bay. He crosses the Alberta-Saskatchewan border and continues west through the Battle River Valley, angling southeast to Red Deer River at Buffalo Lake and on to the Bear Hills. From there, he goes eastwards via Wetaskiwin to Edmonton and along the banks of the North Saskatchewan to the mouth of the Sturgeon River. By the time he gets back to York Factory, Henday has covered 4000 kilometres in 52 weeks.

THE FUR TRADE MAKES THE NATIVES GIDDY

Tribal Trade

The first "export" trade route out of the province is a First Nations' affair. The Blackfoot sell their catch of bison and beaver furs to the Cree, who then make the backbreaking trip by canoe down the Saskatchewan River to sell them at Hudson Bay.

The First Fort

The fur traders decide they want to cut out the Cree middlemen and build a series of forts from which to trade. In 1778, the North West Company's Fort Chipewyan, near the mouth of the Athabasca River, becomes the first. Eventually a network of strong outposts is created throughout the province.

A Place of Learning

Roderick MacKenzie builds a library at Fort Chipewyan in 1790, which eventually houses 2000 books. His cousin Alexander becomes a great discoverer of rivers.

The Race is On

Chipewyan is built for the North West Company in a bid to beat off its rival, the HBC, and secure the West's trades routes. The fort is used as the base from which Alexander Mackenzie sets out on his 1789 expedition to the Arctic Ocean from Lake Athabasca, on the river that now bears his name. A later Mackenzie expedition in 1793 up the Peace River and across the Rockies discovers the first overland route to the Pacific Ocean.

MACKENZIE TRAVELS THE NORTH

Mackenzie's Mission

The 1793 discovery fulfils Mackenzie's dream to find a cross-Canada route from Eastern Canada to the Pacific. Eventually Mackenzie charts a pathway known as The Alexander Mackenzie Voyageur Route, 8500 kilometres in length. The route starts at the old port of Québec, Québec City, and goes to Alexander Mackenzie Provincial Park, on the north shore of Dean Channel, west of Bella Coola. Along the way are located 140 communities, two World Heritage Sites, two national parks, five Heritage Rivers, six National Historic Sites/Parks and numerous provincial parks, reserves, historic sites and regional/community heritage resources.

Checking It Out

HBC men Philip Turnor and Peter Fidler are hired by the British Government to conduct the first survey of the Athabasca and Slave areas in 1790.

Making A Big Point

In 1991, the town of Elk Point, 250 kilometres east of Edmonton, commemorates the bicentennial anniversary of the first settlement on that spot by erecting a 10-metre-high statue of its oldest visitor, explorer/fur trader Peter Fidler. The Fidler statue is carved out of wood with a chainsaw and can be found at the northern end of town.

DID YOU KNOW?

Herman Poulin is the creative genius behind Fidler's statue. He is also responsible for Bonnyville's 7-metre-high statue of Angus Shaw (the first European to set foot in that area, in the mid-1700s) and the 4-metre-tall roadside attraction that depicts David Thompson landing on the shores of Lac La Biche in a canoe.

Bitter Rivals on Rivers and on Land

The HBC's first trading post in Alberta, Buckingham House, is built in 1792—beside the North West Company's Fort George. The two sites can be visited today, 13 kilometres southeast of Elk Point on Highway 646. In 1795, the HBC builds Edmonton House, located near present-day Fort Saskatchewan on the Saskatchewan River, a month before the North West Company build rival Fort Augustus. In 1817, rivalry is so intense the two companies' forts at Lesser Slave Lake are built only 200 metres from each other.

Fort-Fest

Rocky Mountain House goes up in 1799. In the next few years, forts spring up all over the place.

Burning Bright

In 1798, a blacksmith at Fort Edmonton is the first to use coal in Alberta to fire his furnace.

Mountain High

The North West Company builds the first supply post in the Rockies in 1813, on Brule Lake. It later becomes known as Jasper House after clerk Jasper Hawes, the man who built it.

Yellow Legacy

In 1820, Iroquois trader Pierre Bostonnais guides HBC explorers through the northern Rockies. His light-coloured hair wins him the nickname "Tête Jaune" (Yellowhead) from which the Trans-Canada Highway gets its name. The highway opens officially in 1970.

Fight for the Fur Trade

By 1821, the HBC wins out over the North West Company, and the two amalgamate. The HBC name is retained and the "new" company bans trading liquor for Native furs. But many traders do it anyway.

The West Opens Up

Alberta's oldest westward travel route is the 1500-kilometre-long route from Winnipeg to Edmonton, that follows the course of the North Saskatchewan River.

Making Tracks

George Simpson, a Scot, is the man appointed by the HBC to make the company leaner and more efficient after its merger with the North West Company in 1821. He cuts costs by laying off staff at posts across the West.

Making Tracks

George Simpson also cuts Alberta's first road in 1824, the first deliberately cut pack trail in the province. The route follows an old Indian portage trail connecting Edmonton to Fort Assiniboine (located 120 kilometres northeast of Edmonton on the Athabasca River, near present-day Whitecourt). Thus Edmonton becomes an important stop on the first cross-Canada route from the east to the west coast.

The Road to Hell

In 1846, artist Paul Kane describes the Edmonton-Assiniboine Trail as "almost impassable, being wet and swampy, and the horses often stuck fast and threw off their loads in an effort to extricate themselves from the mire."

Commercial Governance

The Hudson's Bay Company charter granting exclusive rights to trade in the Canadian North-West is renewed in 1837 on condition that the company promote religious and moral advancement.

MISSIONARIES FOLLOW IN HBC FOOTSTEPS

Men on a Mission

Reverend Robert Rundle is the first missionary to arrive in Alberta at Fort Edmonton in 1840, where he sets up the first Methodist Mission. The next is built at Pigeon Lake in 1947, where the first garden planted outside a western Canadian fort thrives.

Not too Far Behind

Jean-Baptiste Thibault becomes Alberta's first Roman Catholic missionary. He arrives at Lac Ste. Anne in 1842. The Catholics convert many Métis and aboriginals in the northern part of the province.

A Piece of the Action

In 1849, the HBC faces its first challenge when a committee of First Nations, Métis, Protestant and Catholic religious leaders challenge its exclusive trade restrictions, eventually leading to the disintegration of HBC rule.

The First Offspring

Jean-Baptiste Lagimodière, a French HBC employee, and his wife Marie-Anne have the first white child born in wedlock in the West. Their son René is born in Pembina in January 1808. The Lagimodières' sixth child, Julie, became the mother of Louis Riel, the Métis insurgent who lead the Métis rebellions of 1870 and 1885.

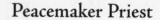

Peacemaker Priest

Father Albert Lacombe arrives in Edmonton in 1852 and is credited with keeping the peace with the Aboriginals in the area. Later Lacombe becomes the first parish priest in the growing settlement of Calgary.

Mission Accomplished

Lacombe's dream is to create communities where he can teach the Aboriginals to farm and educate their children. He is eventually granted a 21-year lease on four townsites, St. Paul des Métis, St. Boniface, Prince Albert and St. Albert in 1865.

Religious Foundation

St. Albert, named after Father Lacombe (not the province), is established four years before the Lacombe's lease is granted, in 1861. The settlement is the first non-fortified community in Alberta and the largest agricultural settlement west of Winnipeg. The settlement develops into the city of St. Albert, Edmonton's adjoining city.

Mission Failed

Although St. Paul des Métis fails in its early days as a Native settlement because it is so isolated, it is revived by a new wave of non-Native settlers in 1905. Under the name St. Paul, the hamlet thrives to achieve village status in 1912. The railway arrives in 1920, electricity in 1921 and natural gas in 1949.

Women Spread the Word

Alberta s first nuns, The Grey Nuns, arrive from Montréal and take up residence at the Lac Ste. Anne Mission in 1859. The nuns soon join the Oblate Mission at Lac La Biche, 220 kilometres northeast of Edmonton. The town becomes a religious centre and a warehouse for the storage of supplies for all the northern missions. With the arrival of the railroad in 1910, the future prosperity of the town is secured.

Better Late Than Never
The Church of England's first missionary to Alberta, William Newton, arrives in 1874.

Just a Trickle

By 1870, there are still only a dozen permanent settlements in Alberta, and most of these are only trading posts or missions.

Caught in the Rain
In 1874, hundreds of Métis out on a hunting trip get caught in a disastrous prairie storm and die.

Excellent Prospects

Father Jean-Baptiste Morin brings Franco-Americans from the U.S. state of Kansas to populate the town of Vegreville (located near Beaver Hill Lake, 88 kilometres east of Edmonton). By 1895, a post office and a French school is built, and a Catholic church by 1904.

Honourable Predecessor

Vegreville is named for Father Valentin Végreville, a French Oblate priest, who served as a missionary in the province for half a century. Végreville spoke several aboriginal languages. He dies in 1903 without ever visiting the community that bears his name.

U.S. WHISKEY POSTS TRADE IN VIOLENCE

Whiskey Traders

At the end of the U.S. Civil War, in 1866, American toughs wander into the Canadian West. Among them are whiskey traders looking north for new markets. Although laws in both countries make it illegal to sell liquor to First Nations in the North-West Territories, there is no police force to stop them.

DID YOU  **KNOW?**

"Whiskey" with an "e" means the brew originally comes from Ireland. "Whisky" without an "e" means the drink comes from Scotland.

Let's Live a Little

The whiskey traders set up trading posts and name them aptly. Fort Whoop-Up in Lethbridge has 11 log cabins in 1869 and becomes the focal point for the liquor trade. The First Nations burn the buildings down, so 32 men are employed for four years to build a massive fort that cost $25,000. In its first year of operation, the fort makes a profit of $50,000.

Firewater Flows

This easy cash spawns a network of strangely named liquor outlets: Fort Stand-Off, where the Belly and Waterton Rivers meet; Fort Spitzee on High River and Fort Slide-Out, so-called because the men planned to "slide out" in the face of an attack.

A Lawless Road

By 1860, the Whoop-Up Trail starts at Fort Benton in Montana, and goes northwards to Calgary via Fort Macleod, becoming a major route for guns, tobacco and whiskey to be traded for First Nation's furs.

The Price of Life

Humanity took a tumble among these men out to make a profit by any means necessary. A letter from one whiskey trader states:

Dear friend,

My partner Will Geary got to putting on airs and I shot him dead. The potatoes is looking well.

Yours truly,
Skookum Jim

Hijacking the Hooch

The NWMP pull the plug on the last whiskey trader in the Blackfoot region, putting J.D. Weatherwax out of business on February 17, 1875.

Room Service

In the 1880s, the Macleod Hotel, at Fort Macleod, has a sign up to welcome visitors that reads "Towels changed only once a week; every known fluid sold at the bar except water; baths furnished free down at the river; assaults on cook strictly forbidden; and all guests must rise by 6:00 AM as the bedsheets are needed for tablecloths."

GO WEST, YOUNG (NWMP) MEN

Lawless West

An expedition in 1872 recommends the creation of a military-style force to police the West, in danger of being overrun by bands of renegade U.S. fur and whiskey traders.

Mañana, Mañana

But Canada's first prime minister, Sir John A. Macdonald, known as an arch procrastinator and given the nickname "Old Tomorrow," delays the creation of the force for financial reasons. That changes when a group of U.S. wolf-hunters brutally murder a band of Indians in a tragic event known as the Cypress Hills Massacre. The NWT's lieutenant-governor is most displeased and forces Macdonald to set up a force.

Ride 'em Out

In 1873, 275 members of the North-West Mounted Police set out from Manitoba on a 1280-kilometre trek into the lawless West. Virtually none have any experience, their guns are obsolete, and their tents blow away in the wind.

For Glory Not Cash

The policemen are paid as little as 75 cents a day but are bought by promises of a quarter section (65 hectares) of land after three years of service.

Iron Man

The man who turns the NWMP into a force to be reckoned with is the aptly named Sam Steele. As a sergeant-major, he is a ruthless trainer—so tough that when his own brother Dick is thrown by a horse and kicked for good measure, Steele unsympathetically orders his "lout" of a brother to be carried off the parade square.

Parched Police

As the cops trek West they run out of water and end up having to drink diluted bison urine. The mosquitoes are so thick they extinguish campfires by sheer weight of numbers. Horses die from starvation and so do the men.

A Pott of Gold

The force survives its first year, thanks to Jerry Potts, a Métis scout and guide. Potts knows the prairie like the back of his hand. His skill and bravery are unequalled on the Canadian plains. Potts serves the Mounties for 22 years.

Cop Shops

In 1874, the Mounties build their headquarters at Fort Macleod. A police post in Calgary breaks ground on August 18.

Spirited Away

Within a year, without firing a shot, the Mounties arrest or scare off the renegades and virtually wipe out the whisky trade.

Thanks, But No Thanks

The government's token of appreciation for the Mounties' work? A pay cut down to 40 cents a day and no land!

THE BLACKFOOT MEET THE GREENHORNS

Gratitude in Chief

But the real thanks for a peaceful settlement of the West go to Chief Crowfoot of the Blackfoot. Although his people are reduced by alcohol, smallpox and the disappearance of the bison, Crowfoot keeps the peace among his people and manages to avoid a copy of the U.S.'s mass slaughter of Natives.

Entreating Goodwill

Crowfoot, with other Blood, Piegan, Sarcee and Stony chiefs, Commissioner David Laird and Lieutenant-Colonel James Macleod sign Treaty No. 7 on September 23, 1877, at Blackfoot Crossing. The First Nations receive 69,039 km^2 for their reserves and $12 for each tribe member.

Cannibal

The first person to be legally executed under the Mounties' jurisdiction is Swift Runner, a cannibal. He confesses to eating his mother, brother and six children during a particularly harsh winter. He hangs on December 20, 1879—it is –42°C, and the murderer s last act is to berate the executioner for keeping him waiting so long in the cold.

Murdered Mountie

The first Mountie murdered is Constable M. Greyburn who is shot in the back in the Cypress Hills in 1879. Whodunit remains a mystery.

THE QUEEN AND HER WARDS

On the Warpath

In 1876, Chief Sitting Bull flees to Canada after wiping out General Custer and the 7th Cavalry at the Battle of Little Big Horn. With the bison gone, the group of 500 nearly starve to death before crossing back over the border to the U.S., where the Chief is imprisoned on a reservation and eventually killed by his own people.

In Our Care

The 1876 Indian Act supersedes all previous laws relating to the First Nations and effectively makes them wards of the state.

Reserving the Right

Alberta's first treaty is signed in 1876. Treaty No. 6 leads to the creation of the Saddle Lake and Whitefish Lake Indian reserves, near St. Paul.

Big Blood

Red Crow, the chief of the Blood tribe, is one of the few who initially refuses to sell the tribe's land to the whites. He eventually relents, and the Blood Reserve, near Lethbridge, becomes the largest in Canada in terms of land area. The reserve is set up in 1883, six years after the signing of Treaty 7 in 1877.

The Treaty Legacies

Other First Nation reserves are established for the Blackfoot near Gleichen, the Blood near Cardston, the Peigan near Pincher Creek, the Sarcee near Calgary, and the Stony near Morley.

Meeting our Maker

Traditionally, the First Nations' dead are not buried. Tribes living in the Sand Hills region place them on the ground and cover them with tipis, accompanied by articles for their trip to the spirit world. It is also customary for older aboriginals to visit the "village of the dead" (cemeteries) to talk to their ancestors' spirits. Traditional Natives believe the person's soul stays attached to a person's skeleton, so woe betide anyone moving their graves and thus creating lost souls.

GOOD GRASS BRINGS JOHN WARE TO ALBERTA

Milking Time

The first cattle used for meat arrive in the province in the 1850s. Twenty-five years later, in 1875, cowboys Joe McFarland and Henry Olson deliver Alberta's first herd of diary cows to Fort Macleod, to provide milk for the members of the North-West Mounted Police.

Lariats' Land

In 1876, John Ware becomes one of the first cowboys to settle in Alberta. He comes from the U.S.

The Golden Years

Ware enjoys the halcyon ranching days in the Prairies of 1875–1905, when one million acres (over 400,000 hectares) of land can be leased for less than one cent per acre per year.

Rags to Riches

Ware, born a slave, makes his way to Alberta with Texas Longhorn cattle, which he later breeds successfully in Canada. Ware also pioneers the development of modern rodeo competitions—he could allegedly stop a steer head-on and pull it to the ground, thus inventing the sport of steer wrestling 20 years before the start of the Calgary Stampede.

A Force to be Reckoned With

By 1885, Ware is a successful rancher with a herd of over 200 cattle and an enviable reputation, respected by everyone he meets. The First Nations call him "Matoxy Sex Apee Quin" ("Bad Black White Man") because of his courage and legendary strength.

DID YOU KNOW?

Alberta's first ranching operation starts in 1876. It is owned by George Emerson and located near Fort Macleod.

First Bite

In 1881, the first grazing lease in the province is issued to the Cochrane Ranche Company Limited. Cochrane paid $500,000 for a large tract of land between the Bow River and the CPR line to Calgary. In 1887, 16,600 hectares of the original lease is purchased outright and turned into the Cochrane Ranche, 39 kilometres west of Calgary. This ranch became one of the most successful ranches in the West.

The Big Guys
A few big ranchers, Fred Stimson, George Lane and A.J. McLean, and the beef processor Pat Burns dominate Alberta's cow industry in its early years. Stimson creates the North-West Cattle Company in 1882.

Great Herds
Cattle on the Canadian range grow from 15,000 in 1881 to 110,500 in 1889.

The First Stagecoach

Stagecoach service starts in 1881, run by Max Brouilette, from Coal Banks (now Lethbridge) through Fort Macleod to Pincher Creek.

Signing your Life Away

At a meeting in the Cypress Hills, Big Bear is the last of the Plains Cree chiefs to sign Treaty No. 6 on December 8, 1882.

Raising the Bar

The Bar U, owned by Fred Stimson, becomes the best-managed ranch on the prairies. It declares profits of $133,000 in 1886.

When Hell Freezes Over

A terrible winter in 1886–87 kills 60 percent of some cattle herds. Ranchers decide to build up hay stocks for winter feed in hopes of avoiding future deaths.

Bad Boy

Ernest Cashel, a Kansas-born outlaw, is convicted of murdering a Lacombe rancher. He escapes from police custody twice but is hanged in Calgary in 1904.

Chinese Revolutionary

When Maurice "Two Gun" Cohen, a Calgary gambler and heavy drinker, knocks out a villain trying to rob a Chinese restaurant he wins the respect of the Chinese community. With their support he ends up moving to China to raise money for that country's war effort against the Japanese invaders of 1937. He becomes body-guard to the father of the Chinese Republic, Sun Yat-sen.

CALGARY STAMPEDE: SOME EXCITEMENT

Ride 'em, Cowboy

The first Calgary Stampede shoots out of the stocks in 1912, a six-day rodeo extravaganza with $100,000 in prizes. Guy Weadick is the brains behind it. But the Stampede, which today attracts more tourists than any other event in Alberta, almost never happened.

Moving On

Homesteaders were taking over the rancher's grazing lands, so Weadick's Wild West rodeo was proposed as a swan song good-bye for the cowboys and their trade. But, with funding secured from the "Big Four" (beef processor Pat Burns, ranchers George Lane and Archie McLean, and brewery owner A.E. Cross). Weadick promises to "make Buffalo Bill's Wild West extravaganza look like a sideshow."

One Man Wins

Tom Three Persons, a Blood, wins the world's bucking-horse championship at the first Calgary Stampede—the only Canadian to win a top award.

Behind Every Good Man

There's a great woman. And much of Guy Weadick's success as a vaudeville-performing cowboy is owed to his partner—his wife Flores La Due (born Grace Bensell). As a young girl, Grace runs away to join the circus, then works with famous cowboy Will Rogers for a while before meeting and marrying Weadick with whom she tours all over the world.

Winner in her Own Right

Flores wins the title of World Champion, Trick and Fancy Rope at that first Calgary Stampede, an event she co-organizes with her husband. In 1920, Flores and Guy buy Stampede Ranch in the foothills of the Rocky Mountains—she runs the place while Guy is in charge of "special projects."

Royal Trainer

It is Flores who teaches Edward, Prince of Wales (later King Edward VIII), to ride a horse properly, when he buys the nearby E.P. Ranch.

Bronco Success...Nearly

Although 40,000 spectators turn up to the 1912 rodeo premiere (Calgary's population at the time is only 50,000), and the Stampede makes a profit, the second rodeo isn't staged until after WWI is over, in 1919. It becomes an annual event in 1932 with its own grounds and from that day on is billed as the "Greatest Show on Earth."

 DID YOU KNOW?

Both Guy Weadick and Flores La Due are buried in High River—the birthplace of Prime Minister Joe Clark.

PAT BURNS:
A MEATPACKER FROM
WAY BACK

Locked up for Lunch

By 1906, the halcyon days of ranching are done and dusted.
Cattle are no longer free to roam freely. By 1912, farmers begin
to grow their own feed, such as barley and oats, on land adjoining their cattle ranches and build "feedlots," huge pens with
feeding troughs, to keep and feed the cattle in.

Early Empire

By 1910, Pat Burns' ranching and farming empire covers an area
of 180,000 hectares, nearly 2000 km². He runs a "vertically
integrated" business, controlling every step of the industrial process, from breeding cattle, feeding them in the new "feedlots,"
(about 30,000 at a time), packing the meat and distributing it
through his chain of stores.

Meat Magnet

But Burns, the man who made millions out of packing and distributing cattle loses his plant, the biggest in western Canada, to
a 1912 blaze. Firemen try to conquer the inferno in temperatures
of −35°C. Losses of $1 million in property damage and scorched
carcasses are incurred.

Enduring Legacy

Started in 1987, the annual Cowboy Gathering whoops it up
every summer at Pincher Creek in an effort to keep cowboy
culture alive. Over four days, cowboy poetry (free-ranging
rhyming poetry that depict humorous and hearty tales of ranching, farming and the rodeo), country and western music shows,
food, rodeos, a fair and fun can be had by all.

THE SEEDS OF ALBERTA AGRICULTURE

The First White Man to Till the Earth
This accolade goes to fur trader Peter Pond who plants a garden near Lake Athabasca in 1779. He also builds the first house.

If at First You Don't Succeed
A.N. McLeod builds Alberta's second house at Fort McMurray, in 1786.

Sowing Seeds
Wheat is first grown near Lac La Biche, one of Alberta's oldest communities, in 1798.

Ready to Settle Down
In 1872, homesteaders are offered 65 hectares of free land in the Dominion Land Act. The offer, available to the heads of families and to single male adults, is made on condition of:

- payment of a $10 registration fee,
- residing on the land for three years,
- cultivating 12 hectares and
- building a permanent dwelling.

Kicking Along
George Palliser's expedition arrives in 1858 to survey the prairies and make plans for the railroad. During the trip, the group's geologist, Dr. James Hector, falls off his kicking horse and is knocked unconscious. The pass where he fell is named the Kicking Horse Pass and later becomes part of the route taken by the Canadian Pacific Railway to cross the Rocky Mountains.

THE CALGARY– EDMONTON CORRIDOR: A DENSE PLACE TO LIVE

A Prosperous Corridor

By 1875, a 312-kilometre-long south-north route has been forged between Calgary and Edmonton following an ancient glacial corridor. The trail really develops when Methodist missionaries build a mission at Morley and cut a formidable path to it from Fort Edmonton, through Red Deer, and on to Lone Pine, 45 kilometres farther south. Later the HBC finish off the job to Calgary.

A Dense Place to Live
By 2005, the Calgary–Edmonton corridor has become the most urbanized area in Alberta and one of the most densely populated in Canada

Mountain Pass
Surveyor Sanford Fleming declares, in 1872, the Crowsnest Pass is the preferable railway route through the Canadian Rockies.

Coast to Coast

The Canadian Parliament in Ottawa creates the Canadian Pacific Railway (CPR) to connect BC to Eastern Canada, a promise made as a condition of BC joining Confederation in 1871.

Government Grant

Ottawa gives the CPR a $25 million grant and 100,000 km^2 of land "fairly fit for settlement" on the prairies to encourage the completion of a rail link.

The Road North

The Athabasca Landing Trail is first blazed in 1877 to allow carts to travel northwards 160 kilometres from Edmonton. The trail is cleared with axes, and corduroy is laid onto the soggiest areas of muskeg. By 1906, thousands of settlers use it on their way to Peace River Country.

From the Emerald Isle

Irish-born John Glenn is the first European to settle Calgary in 1873 with his wife Adelaide. They build a small log cabin where Fish Creek and the Bow River meet. Glenn builds the province's first irrigation system by damming the Macleod River with stones and rocks and diverting it into his fields.

A Sparse Population

By 1881, the *Edmonton Bulletin* reports that only 363 settlers have built homes between Calgary and Edmonton.

Town Planning

A Mr. Kettles lays out plans for the present-day town of Pincher Creek in 1882.

Iron Horse Comes West

The first train steams west from Saskatchewan, going through Medicine Hat to Fort Calgary, on August 9, 1883—then the settlement of present-day Alberta begins.

Making Tracks

The same year, on August 11, the first train crosses the Elbow River at Fort Calgary. By December 2, a full passenger service is up and running between Winnipeg and Calgary.

Namesake for a Nipper
John Calgary Costello becomes the first child of European descent born in Calgary on November 19, 1883.

From Siding to Springs

Siding No. 29 is renamed Banff by Lord Strathcona, for the Scottish royal burgh of Banff in 1883.

Fields of Plenty
Sam Lucas establishes the first experimental farm in the North-West Territories, 9 kilometres north of Wetaskiwin in 1883.

Canmore's Coal

Established in 1883, Canmore grows as a coal-mining town, servicing the needs of the railroad as it makes its way westward into the Canadian Rockies. Canmore remains an active coal-mining community until 1979, but today it booms as a time-share tourist town amid mountains of stunning natural beauty.

Conceited Namesake
Canmore is named in honour of Malcolm of Canmore, the king of Scotland from 1057 to 1093. The translation of the name is "big head."

DID YOU KNOW?

In 1884, sheep are banned from roaming any farther south than the Highwood River.

More Trains

Lethbridge and Medicine Hat get connected by light-gauge railway in 1885.

The First Mormons

Mormons arrive in 1884 to settle the south of the province and are joined a couple of years later by Utah leader Charles Ora Card. His mission is to find a place of "peace and asylum" and safe place to practice polygamy. Card and his clan settle happily on a site between the Belly and St. Mary Rivers and set up their own town, called surprise, surprise, Cardston!

Skilled Imports
Chinese labourers are responsible for building the West's railways. In the peak construction year of 1883, 6000 to 7500 Chinese work on various sections of track.

Blue Blood Tax

Once the track is finished in 1885 the Chinese labourers aren't wanted anymore, so to deter them settling, and any more coming, a $50 head tax is imposed, making it painfully expensive for a Chinese immigrant to buy his family's passage. The community became a society of bachelors.

The Cheek of It
The head tax is increased in 1900 to $100, and again in 1903 to $500—the equivalent of two years' wages. In total the Government collects $23 million in head taxes.

Disgraceful Racists

In 1923, Canada's new Chinese Immigration Act excludes all but a handful of Chinese from immigrating to Canada. And just to rub salt in the wound, the Act is introduced on Dominion Day, July 1, which the Chinese community dub "Humiliation Day." They refuse to celebrate Dominion Day for years to come. The law remains on the statute books until its repeal in 1948 and in that time only 50 Chinese immigrate to Canada.

Rivals United

On July 21, 1889, a crowd of 21,000 turns up to watch ground being broken for the new Calgary and Edmonton Railway. It takes two years, until July 27, 1891, to complete, but the railway cuts the five-day stagecoach ride down to three hours by train. The first train from Calgary arrives at the new station, on Whyte Avenue, south Edmonton, on August 10.

The Network is Born

The Crowsnest Pass Railway begins in 1897, and the Canadian Northern Railway reaches Edmonton in 1905. By 1916, the Edmonton, Dunvegan and British Columbia Railway reaches Peace River, and in 1925 the A&GW Railway arrives at Fort McMurray.

A Real Model Farm

In 1891, the government funds a model farm in Lethbridge that later evolves into the Lethbridge Research Centre, the largest experimental agricultural facility in Canada.

Here They Come

German-born Ukrainians settle Medicine Hat in 1889. Next come the first Austro-Hungarian settlers by train in 1891, followed by a trainload of Russian Ukrainians two months later.

God on Our Side

A colony of German Moravians homestead 48 kilometres east of Edmonton (in present-day Lamont County) in 1894. They build the first Moravian Church in western Canada, and name the village Bruderheim, which translates as "Home of the Brethren."

The Capital of God

Lamont County has more churches per capita than anywhere
else in North America, 47 of them, onion-domed spires of the
Ukrainian Orthodox Church and Eastern Rite Churches built
by settlers from the former Austro-Hungarian provinces of
Galicia and Bukovyna.

Population Boom Boom Boom

Alberta's population explodes. (These numbers don't include the
First Nations population.)

1881	1000
1891	17,500
1901	73,000
1911	274,000
1921	584,000

Chick and Guy Magnet

As a result of a campaign started in 1897 by Canada's minister
of the interior, Clifford Sifton, to entice settlers to come over the
water, the population of Alberta grows eightfold in two decades.
The settlers are mostly from Britain, the U.S., Germany, the
Ukraine, Romania and Ontario.

Prize PR

Sifton's marketing tactics are so successful the ploy attracts over two million settlers of "good quality" to "the golden fields" in Canada. It has been hailed as the most successful public-relations campaign in Canadian history.

Good-Quality Discrimination

But not everyone was welcome. British, German and Scandinavian stock are highly thought of, but Eastern Europeans are considered economically backward, religiously superstitious and politically deferential. And Minister of the Interior Sifton orders that "No steps are to be taken to assist or encourage Italian immigration to Canada."

Viva Italia

But the need for farmers and labourers who can survive the terrible prairie winters forces the government to take another look. George Burns, a CPR agent, puts it this way in 1904: "Italians are the only class of labour we can employ who can live for a year on the wages they earn in six months…if we have the Italians…there is no danger of their jumping their jobs and leaving us in the lurch."

Homecoming

Between 1901 and 1905, approximately 40,000 homesteads are granted to future Albertans. A homestead is approximately a quarter-section (65 hectares) of developed or undeveloped land.

DID YOU KNOW?

By 1901, 6000 U.S. citizens live in Alberta.

A Jewel in the Wilderness

Edmond Brosseau, a Québecois, comes to Alberta to pan for
gold and ends up in a hamlet 160 kilometres northeast of
Edmonton that eventually takes his name. Cree previously knew
the location of the hamlet as *Matapeskuteweyak* ("the prairie
which comes out of the river"). The Cree, Chipewyan and
Blackfoot Nations have used the river as a crossing for thousands
of years. Father Albert Lacombe tries to establish a mission here
in 1864, but it is abandoned six years later.

Transportation Dependent

By 1907, Brousseau is thriving with a school, a general store,
a livery barn, a jewellery and watch repair store, a blacksmith's
and a fine hotel that boasts a unique two-storey privy. But by the
1930s, the town is in decline—bypassed by both the CPR and
the new highway nearby.

The Earth Provides

In Drayton Valley, located between the Pembina and North
Saskatchewan Rivers, homes are made out of spruce or pine logs,
hewn with broad axes. Hand-hewn pine or cedar shingles are
used for the roof, and mud plaster is slapped on exterior walls for
insulation each fall.

Tough without Modern Luxuries

Interior stoves soon become a problem because they often catch
fire. But the problem is eventually solved with brick chimneys.
Lighting comes from coal oil in lamps.

Basic Farming

Most fields are cleared with plows pulled by horses or oxen.
Crop rotation starts immediately, and grass or clover is planted
every three years to re-invigorate the soil with nitrogen. The
main crops grown by the first homesteaders are the principal
crops still grown today—oats, barley, rye, clover and wheat.

Animal Menu

Much of the grain is used to feed livestock. The cost of a bushel of wheat in 1905 is 50 cents, a bushel of oats cost 5 to 20 cents, and Dutch clover, $1.00 per pound (about half a kilogram).

As British as a Bulldog

Lloydminster is established in 1903 by 2600 Barr colonists arriving directly from the British Isles. They intend to create an exclusively British, alcohol-free utopia. The settlement is named for Anglican Bishop George Lloyd, the Barr Colony's leader and a strong temperance advocate.

Split Personality

Lloydminster straddles the border of Saskatchewan and Alberta when both become provinces in 1905. In 1994, to mark its unique bi-provincial status, the city erects a monument consisting of four 30-metre-tall orange survey markers near the city's downtown core. The markers denote the Fourth Meridian of the Dominion Land Survey, 110° west longitude.

Lovely Lethbridge

In 1910, 5000 homestead applications are filed at the Lethbridge land office.

Build and They Will Come

From 1906 to 1913, real estate agent and developer Fred Lowes makes $6 million exploiting the property boom in Calgary and Edmonton. At any given time he has 5000 of the best agricultural parcels and more than 20,000 km^2 listed for sale. But he expands too fast, holds millions in mortgages and loses his fortune almost overnight at the outbreak of WWI. Lowes dies penniless in a mental institution in 1950.

Prairie Tracks United

To mark completion of the Canadian Northern Railway from Winnipeg to Edmonton, Alberta Lieutenant-Governor G. Bulyea drives home a silver spike into the track on November 24, 1905.

Summer Jobs

The CPR schedule special harvesters' excursion trains offering reduced fares for able-bodied seasonal workers travelling to Alberta and Saskatchewan to harvest the "granary of the world."

Grouard Growing

By the late 1800s, Grouard, on the northwest side of Lesser Slave Lake where it meets the Sweet Heart River, is the largest settlement beyond the Athabasca River. Settlers are attracted by fertile farmland in the Peace River Valley. By 1910, the town has 447 residents (one-tenth of Peace River Country's total population), three stores, a hospital and a Dominion land office. But the trip to Edmonton still takes around 25 days.

Careless Critters

But by 1893, the earliest gold prospectors using the Edmonton-Athabasca Trail get into serious trouble with the First Nations. The prospectors are using poisoned bait to catch game, which also proves deadly to the tribes' dogs. Tensions rise and the NWMP are called in to keep the peace. In 1898, they set up a regional headquarters in Grouard.

Commemorative Ride

In 1973, 19 horse-riders celebrate the 100th anniversary of the NWMP's arrival in Alberta (1873), by taking the first organized tourist tour of the Grouard-Peace River Trail.

The Cost of Finding Peace
The price tag for a journey from Grouard to the Peace River Crossing (190 kilometres) in 1905 is $25 per person including 68 kilograms of freight. Extra baggage carries a $5 charge per 45 kilograms.

That's Progress

In 1913, A.M. Bezanson drives a 40-horsepower Cadillac on the same Grouard–Peace River route and cuts the journey to eight hours from the nine days taken in the decades before.

Sunken Road
In 1907, Lesser Slave Lake dries up and the government lays a road across it. But the water comes back and today no one knows the exact location of this old road.

Available and Arable

By 1908, the fertile lands in the northwestern areas of the Peace River Valley are the only arable lands as yet unfarmed.

The Last Great West
To aid settlement, the railway is extended to Edson, Yellowhead Country, in 1910. Land is available for $10 for 65 hectares.

The Last Great Push
A new trail, 300 kilometres long, is cut through the landscape from Edson northwest to Grande Prairie, one of Alberta's first roads to be cut through the bush on a large scale, complete with bridges and ferries. It is completed in 1911, by which time Edson is thriving with stores and a five-star hotel.

Not so Grand

By comparison, Grande Prairie in 1911 has one restaurant and one blacksmith, owned and operated by the town's only resident, William Bredin. Farmers come to work during the summer and return to Edmonton in winter.

A Laugh Along the Way

American travellers taking the Edson–Grande Prairie trail leave a bittersweet totem to the route's treacherous conditions. They carve a face on a spruce tree, adding a pipe in his mouth for effect, grass for his hair and top it with a hat and an epitaph that reads: "Uncle Sam, died of mud fever on the Edson Trail, 1911."

From Stage to Tracks

J.B. Taft opens up a stagecoach service from Edson to Grande Prairie in 1911, but the tree stumps en route made the ride nearly impassable. The arrival of the Edmonton, Dunvegan and British Columbia Railway in 1916 kills the trail anyway.

Frenchville

Catholic missionary Father Albert Lacombe establishes a French-speaking town, Rouleauville, in present-day Calgary, with its own school, hospital and church, in 1907, in the neighbourhood now known as Mission. But nearby English-speaking residents of Calgary don't take kindly to *les Français* and won't share vital facilities such as the sewage system. Within years, the tiny French town is abandoned.

Nous Sommes Ici

By 1916, approximately 25,000 French Canadians live in Alberta, mostly in Edmonton. In 1925, Francophones set up the Association Canadienne-Française de l'Alberta (ACFA) to safeguard and promote French culture.

Nicely Settled In

By World War I, over 400,000 homestead entries have been recorded in Alberta and Saskatchewan.

DID YOU KNOW?

For a corner lot in downtown Calgary, the price tag in 1883 is $450. A house lot outside the city in 1910 costs around $60.

A Bleak Board

In 1911, the Boards of Trade in Strathcona, Calgary, Fort Saskatchewan and Morinville send a petition to Prime Minister Laurier with over 3000 signatures, opposing the entry of any more blacks into the province.

Watering the Fields

The 3.2-kilometre-long Brooks Aqueduct takes two years to build and is completed in 1915. The aqueduct is featured on the city's crest and helps the town develop into a centre for livestock, grain and vegetable farming.

Waterways that Work

The aqueduct is part of a $40-million irrigation scheme created by the CPR to irrigate the southern regions of the province and render them fit for farming. The scheme includes 2140 kilometres of irrigation canals and the Bassano dam.

Colonizing the Plains

The CPR establishes 24 "colonies" across the prairies. These settlements have 762 ready-made farms, each complete with barns, houses, sheds and fences. If settlers can't afford to buy the farms outright, the CPR lends them the money. In tough years, loan payments are deferred. But the icing on the cake are fields that come ploughed, so settlers without farming experience are given a fighting chance.

Canadian Farms Cooler than American

In 1908, the vicinity of present-day Plamondon, 200 kilometres northeast of Edmonton, is populated mostly by Métis. That all changes overnight, when a group of Québecers arrive, disillusioned with life in Michigan. Joseph Plamondon is one of them, having realized that the 65-hectare farms in Canada are much more attractive than 16 hectares and a mule offered in the U.S. Along the way, Plamondon's wife celebrates the birth of their 12th child. Many of the namesake family's descendents still live in the town.

Total Commitment
By 1909, the CPR spends more than the Canadian government on immigration and settling the Prairies. Its headquarters are moved to Calgary in 1912.

Hutterhomers
The first Hutterites in Alberta arrive from North and South Dakota in 1918.

Growing Farmers of the Future

Mr. W.J. Elliott establishes the first rural club for boys and girls in Alberta, in 1917. The clubs evolve into the 4-H clubs of today, so popular among rural youth. Their motto "Learn to Do by Doing" means young farmers and kids in rural areas run the show, meet once a month and organize their own events and fundraisers.

The Proof is in the Pudding Sale

The clubs become so popular that by 1962, 4-H runs and hosts its own four-hour-long TV show. During the 1970s, the organization buys its own land and constructs offices and hostels throughout the province.

Rainman

When a drought hits Medicine Hat in 1921, desperate farmers employ a rainmaker to save them. Two weeks later the skies open up with such a downpour the land is flooded and impossible to sow. Then the drought returns with a vengeance. That year, about 10,000 Alberta farms are abandoned.

United We Stand

Alberta farmers got together in a 1923 cooperative to up their bargaining power and share resources by creating the Alberta Wheat Pool, the first grain pool in North America. Operations begin with 16 participating elevator operators.

By the Wagonload

A joint venture by the Canadian government, the CPR and the CNR in 1925 called the Railway Agreement is established to entice central and eastern European immigrants to Canada. It works. Happy to flee the political and cultural chaos in post-WWI Europe, half the 72,000 immigrants who come to Alberta between 1926 and 1930 are from Central and Eastern Europe.

Salt of the Earth

The village of Mallaig is named after a fishing village in Scotland, in 1928—the same year the railway arrives there. Prosperity there depends on the same backbreaking work demanded in all virgin homesteads across Alberta. According to law, settlers have three years to break 12 hectares of their land, fence their quarter section, and build a house before they can make a formal claim for ownership of the land. Most homesteaders realize the only way to accomplish the task is through cooperation with the community.

Good at the Top
Wheat production peaks in 1928 at 566 million bushels.

Farmers on Fertilizer
The number of farmers in Alberta reaches an all-time peak in 1936 at 99,732.

Dust Bowl

The Great Depression of the 1930s is a terrible time for Alberta. Droughts, grasshopper plagues, soil erosion from freak winds and falling wheat prices make it a true disaster. Many farmers go bankrupt and lose their land. Grain receipts fall from $135 million in 1929 to a paltry $16 million by 1937.

Crash Value

In 1928, the average family income in Alberta is $548. Five years later it drops to $212.

Help at Hand

At the depth of the Depression, one-fifth of Calgary's 75,000 residents exist on welfare. In Edmonton, 13,000 unemployed men gather in the Market Square for a hunger march on December 20, 1932.

Cultural Enclave

In the 1930s, Mennonites settle the town of La Crete, 56 kilometres southwest of High Level. They keep to themselves, farm the land and only open the first post office in 1956. Today most townsfolk speak "Plautdeutsch" or "Low German," but all businesses serve their customers in English as well.

Ranches Remain Big

In 1941, a survey counts the number of ranches in Alberta at 218, with an average land size of about 4000 hectares.

Alberta's Population Growth

1931	731,605
1941	796,169
1951	939,501
1956	1,123,116
1961	1,331,944
1966	1,463,203
1971	1,627,874
1976	1,838,035
1981	2,237,724
1986	2,365,825
1991	2,545,553
1996	2,696,826
2001	2,974,807
2005	3,306,359

(source: Statistics Canada)

Urban Sprawl

From 1946 to 1966, the percentage of the population living on farms is cut by half from 41 percent to 19 percent, and 27 percent of Alberta's population live in Edmonton and Calgary. In 2005, the proportions remain the same as in 1966: 81 percent in urban areas, 19 percent in the country.

As Far as You Can Go

High Level (which today calls itself the "Gateway to the South") is the most northern town in Alberta, 800 kilometres north of Edmonton (which calls itself the "Gateway to the North"). The Beaver Nation, which has populated the High Level region for centuries, cut the first trails and roads to the nearby settlements of Hay Lakes, Meander River further north and Fort Vermilion, 80 kilometres southeast. White men don't really arrive in the area en masse until 1942, when a road is built across the North, and white farmers settle there.

Young and Vibrant

High Level has the distinction of owning the most northerly grain elevators in North America. The town is also home to one of the youngest populations in North America, 50 percent of its 4000 residents are under 25, and most work in thriving forestry and oil-and-gas industries.

Lucrative Lake

Lebanese immigrants settle in the Lac La Biche area in the early 1900s, attracted by mink-farming opportunities. Mink eat fish, found in abundance in the region's 150 lakes. Today the ethnic group numbers 2800—the largest Lebanese per capita population in North America.

From Mink to Motorcars

Today, Albert, son of Lebanese mink farmer Chaffic Mograhrabi, owns the 1672-m² Lac La Biche Sporting Goods store, which sells more Honda ATVs than any other retailer in North America.

Banning Beef

The American government closes the U.S. border to Canadian cattle in 1952 because of an outbreak of foot and mouth disease.

Busting Through the Roof

But it doesn't take long to recover and with increasing mechanization feeding cows more efficiently on Alberta's farms, exports of beef cattle and calves to the US jumps from 6000 in 1956 to 200,000 just two years later.

DID YOU  KNOW?

In 1960, Calgary had 325,000 inhabitants, Edmonton just under 300,000.

Farm Receipts
By 1963, more than half of Alberta's cash income from farming is generated by livestock production.

More Cows than People
In 1970, Alberta boasts nearly 3 million cattle, about half of Western Canada's total and more than one-quarter of Canada's total (11.6 million). Of these, almost half come from small farms less than a section in size. Only 15 percent come from operations of more than 650 hectares in size.

Can You Supersize That Please

Between 1960 and 1972, a massive worldwide increase in grain yields means it is now cheap enough to increase the amount of grain a cow is fed by 55 percent.

Farmers Dance
Descendents of Ukrainian farmers set up their own cultural showcase in 1973, the annual Pysanka Festival. The bill includes a dance festival, grandstand shows, arts and crafts sales and, of course, a lot, a lot of food.

Grateful for Protection
In 1974, the Ukrainian com-munity pay tribute to the NWMP by build-ing them a monu-ment. The world's biggest Easter egg, called a pysanka, sits outside the entrance to the predominantly Ukrainian village of Vegreville.

Tumbling Down

The 1986 oil crisis hits at a time when grain prices are at such a low level that thousands of farms go out of business.

But Cows Continue Chewing the Cud

By the end of the 1980s, Alberta is the largest beef-producing province in Canada, with over 40 percent of the Canadian beef herd. Alberta also slaughters over half the country's cows in nine enormous packing plants, one located in Edmonton, another in High River and seven around Brooks and Calgary.

What Goes Up, Must Come Down

Federal subsidies on rail shipments of grain are axed in 1996 which leads to the shut-down of grain elevators across the prairies.

Super-Super Cattle Restaurant

By 1993, over 4000 feedlots operate in the province with the 100 hundred largest feedlots finishing over half of Alberta's beef cattle. In 1998 feedlot operator Cattleland feeds 25,000 cattle, and Thorlakson Feedyards feeds 18,000 each day.

Going. Going. Gone.

The Calgary Stockyard shuts down in 1989 after more than a century of auctioning cattle to the highest bidder. In its glory years the Stockyard sold an average of 375,000 head annually. Trading in live cattle moves instead to the Chicago Mercantile Exchange, which has been operating since 1964.

GOLD RUSHES AND LOST MINES

Early Birds

The first people to pan for gold visit Edmonton in 1858 on their way to the Fraser River Gold Rush in British Columbia.

It's a Lemon

The Lemon Mine is one of the most enduring legends in Alberta. Frank Lemon and his partner "Blackjack" are reported to have found a gold mine in the Rockies, on the BC side, but are killed, allegedly, by Blackfoot. Rumours emerge later, that it was actually Lemon who killed his partner. Later still, a map is found, reportedly Lemon's. On it, the goldmine is shown on the Alberta side of the mountains. A man called French apparently finds the mine in 1912 but dies when his tent catches fire.

The Gold Rush
In 1896, gold is discovered in the Yukon. Edmonton, the closest town, becomes a staging post for travellers.

The Road to Nowhere
By 1898, the main routes to Dawson City and the Yukon gold rush from Edmonton are 3200 kilometres long. It takes more than six months to make the journey. The Chalmers Route, also known as the "Back-door Trail," starts on the old Edmonton-Fort Assiniboine Trail, then continues to the Athabasca Landing (today's Athabasca) and the Slave Lake settlement (modern-day Grouard). But horses drop like flies, from exhaustion and from munching on poisonous weeds near Swan Hills.

DID YOU  KNOW?

Today's Alaska Highway follows the same route as the Back-door Trail.

Plenty of Warning
An article in the April 1, 1898, issue of the *Klondike News* warns that the route from Edmonton "involves long portages between rivers and lakes and hundreds of miles of travel through an unknown country."

No Prospect for a Lady
The first woman to start on the Klondike Trail is a Mrs. Garner. She gets stranded at Spirit River and never makes it through.

High Price to Pay
Of the 1500 gold seekers who leave Edmonton for the Klondike, an estimated 766 men, nine women and 4000 horses take the overland route to Peace River Crossing (today's Peace River). Only 160 men succeed, but no women, nor horses, make it all the way to the Klondike on this route.

At Any Cost

Six miles out of Fort Assiniboine, near the trail, a baby's grave bears testament to the treacherous conditions the travellers face.

Rotten Moodie
In 1898 and 1899, Inspector J.D. Moodie of the NWMP blazes a government-sponsored trail on a safer route than the Chalmers Route, but the gold rush is already over.

Necessity the Mother of Invention

The inventor of foolproof transportation to get passengers through the treacherous trail north from Edmonton stands to make a fortune. Ergo, the Chicago Steam Sleigh Company builds a tractor to haul heavy supplies, using a spiked steel drum, instead of wheels, that is supposed to provide traction in snow and ice. The drum proved totally useless.

All Things to All Men
Another not-so-ingenious device is Bruno Fabian's amphibious vehicle that is supposed to serve as boat, sleigh and horse-drawn cart all in one. It doesn't work.

Lite Taters

For the journey north, a local brewer invents evaporated pota-toes—lighter to carry than the real thing.

Modern Gold Rush

There is global excitement in 1989 when geological technician Ron Stewart discovers tiny quantities of gold in the Crowsnest Pass near the location of the still-undiscovered Lemon Mine. Prospectors gather there but it turns out to be a total lemon.

PROVINCE OF ALBERTA BLOSSOMS

Territorial Legacy

Princess Louise Caroline Alberta, the sixth child and fourth daughter of Britain's Queen Victoria, visits the province in 1881 with her husband, the Marquis of Lorne, Canada's Governor General from 1878 to 1883. In 1882, the southern portion of the North-West Territories are divided into four districts: Assiniboia, Athabaska, Saskatchewan and Alberta.

Eternally Honoured

The Princess becomes the area's namesake when it becomes a province in 1905. Lake Louise is also named after the princess.

A Token of Love

The Marquis was quite the poet. His dedication to Princess Alberta and the new district reads:

In token for the love which thou has Shown
For this wild land of freedom, I have Named
A Province vast, and for its beauty Famed,
By thy dear name to be hereafter Known.
Alberta shall it be!

Landlocked Birthday

Alberta and Saskatchewan become provinces on the same date—September 1, 1905—and are also the only two of the Canadian provinces and territories without a maritime coast.

Alberta is Born

On September 1, 1905, Prime Minister Sir Wilfrid Laurier addresses a crowd of 15,000 from a specially built ceremonial platform near today's Telus Field, in Edmonton.

A New Hope

Laurier's wish for the new Alberta sums up Canadian national identity: "We do not anticipate, and we do not want, that any individuals should forget the land of their origin or their ancestors," he proclaims, "Let them look to the past, but let them also look to the future; let them look to the land of their ancestors, but let them look also to the land of their children."

Signed, Sealed and Delivered

At 12 noon, a 21-gun salute rings out. George Bulyea is appointed Alberta's first lieutenant-governor, and Alberta officially becomes a province.

Border Boundaries

Alberta is one of only two Canadian provinces to ⌐
one U.S. state. Alberta s U.S. neighbour is Montana. The
is New Brunswick, which has the U.S. state of Maine as its
neighbour: BC is bordered by Washington, Idaho and Montana:
Saskatchewan by Montana and North Dakota: Manitoba by
North Dakota and Minnesota: Québec's American neighbours
are the States of New York, Vermont, New Hampshire and
Maine. Ontario's are Minnesota, Michigan, Ohio, Pennsylvania
and New York. Newfoundland and Labrador, PEI and Nova
Scotia have no U.S. neighbours.

A Big Baby
The new province's boundaries are set at birth to create the following dimensions: the widest portion is 655 kilometres, located
at 53°45'; the narrowest portion is at latitude 49° (the U.S. border)
which is only 290 kilometres; north to south, Alberta is 1200
kilometres long and stretches between the 49th and 60th parallels.

Government First

The province's first election sees the Liberal Party take 22 of
Alberta's 25 seats.

Head Honchos

George Bulyea becomes the first lieutenant-governor, and
Alexander Rutherford, a Liberal, the first premier.

Capital Squabbles

Calgary's population of 11,000 is convinced the city will win out
over Edmonton's 8300 folk to become the new province's capital. But Liberal MP Frank Oliver draws up the electoral boundaries to give the Edmonton area the majority of constituencies.
The choice of Edmonton as the capital city gets the support of
16 of the MLAs and carries the day.

Influence Near the Seat of Power

The Grand Lodge of Alberta, Ancient Free and Accepted
Masons (the Freemasons) is constituted and consecrated on
October 12, 1905. By 1913, there are 72 lodges province-wide.

The First Albertan Political Scandal

Premier Rutherford's power lasts until 1910, when he is forced
to resign over a dodgy government contract awarded to an U.S.
company for building a railway to Fort McMurray.

Power to the Farmers

The United Farmers of Alberta is formed in 1909, a grass-
roots movement to counterbalance the power of bankers and
industrialists.

City Merger

The cities of Edmonton and Strathcona amalgamate into one on
February 1, 1912.

Cities Sprawling

Wetaskiwin becomes Alberta's fifth city in 1906; Red Deer
Alberta's seventh city on March 25, 1913. (Strathcona was
named Alberta's sixth city in 1907.)

Prairie Blooms

The wild rose is chosen as Alberta's official flower in 1930.

Provincial Heraldry

Queen Elizabeth II proclaims Alberta's provincial flag on June 1,
1968. She grants the crest and supporters for Alberta's coat of
arms on July 13, 1982.

THE DAYS OF CHALK AND SLATEBOARDS

Our Way Or the Highway

The first residential school in Alberta, Hospice St. Joseph, opens at Lac La Biche in 1862.

The First School

The first Protestant school west of Manitoba is established by missionary George McDougall in 1864 at Victoria (present-day Pakan). His wife and daughter die in the 1870 smallpox epidemic. On January 25, 1876, George McDougall's body was discovered frozen in the prairie snow, his arms folded across his chest.

The Three First Non-Missionary Educator

Andrew Sibbald is the first schoolteacher in Alberta who is not also a missionary. The missionary McDougall brothers recruit him to teach in Alberta's second school they build at Morley, in 1874. Sibbald Flats and Sibbald Creek in Banff are named after him.

Religious Instruction

A 1882 federal government charter establishes Alberta's first mission school, the Dunbow Industrial School.

School Governors

Authority to make laws regarding education is granted to Alberta's provincial government in 1905. The legislature regulates a system of locally elected public and separate school boards, as well as creates and regulates universities, colleges, technical institutions and other educational forms and institutions.

SOME THINGS STAY THE SAME

Bonne Chance in the North

Bonnyville, in northeastern Alberta, has one of the few all-francophone schools in the province. This is a reflection of the town's population which has the largest concentration of francophones in all the western provinces.

Good Stock

The earliest settlers in Bonnyville arrived in 1907, when missionary Father Thérien convinced four Frenchmen from Beaumont to settle there with their families. The early population was almost entirely French with family names such as Boisvert, Dargis, Hétu, Marcotte, Martel, Mercier, Ouellette and Ouimet. The town is named for the Reverend Father Francis Bonny who arrived in 1908.

Farmers' School

The Alberta Government funds agricultural schools and demonstration farms in Olds, Vermilion and Claresholm in 1913. Olds College today is a world-famous agricultural college with over 550 hectares of experimental gardens and farms. The Vermilion farm evolves into today's Lakeland College.

Let in the Ladies

A residential wing is added to the Claresholm School of Agriculture to accommodate female students in 1922.

Forward-Thinking Schools

Calgary's Southern Alberta Institute of Technology, SAIT, is established in 1916 as North America's first publicly funded post-secondary technical institute. Its counterpart, NAIT, the Northern Alberta Institute of Technology, opens in Edmonton on May 27, 1963.

Frozen Solid

After a three-week closure because of an infantile paralysis (polio) epidemic, Edmonton schools re-open on September 22, 1927. During another epidemic, in 1941, schools closed and lessons were published in newspapers.

Hereditary Genius

Mark McClung, son of suffragette politician Nellie McClung, is named Alberta's Rhodes Scholar for 1935–36.

Wartime Loyalty

Two Jehovah's Witnesses children are expelled from a Lethbridge school for refusing to salute the Canadian flag (the old Union Jack) on October 26, 1943. The children said they believed homage is to be paid only to God, not to material objects.

Rival Cities Get Universities

After 20 years as a satellite branch of the University of Alberta (established in 1907), the University of Calgary becomes fully autonomous in 1966—the same year a university is established in Lethbridge.

Architecture of International Calibre

The University of Lethbridge is one of the most significant examples of modern architecture in Canada. It is the only internationally recognized building in Lethbridge and one of the few in Alberta.

Echoes of Auschwitz

Mayor of Eckville James Keegstra is fired from his school instructor's job and stripped of his teaching certificate in 1984 for instructing his students that the Holocaust was a fraud. He is convicted of crimes of hate speech, given a one-year suspended sentence, a year of probation and ordered to do 200 hours of community service work. He appeals, but the Supreme Court upholds the conviction in a 1990 landmark case.

Jamais Anglais

It took a 10-year battle, but in 1992, francophone parents across Canada win the right to have official language communities self-govern their own schools and set their own curriculum thanks to a campaign waged by Albertan Angeline Martel, a Québec-born sociolinguistics specialist. By 2004, Alberta has 3602 francophone students at 26 schools.

King of the Forests

A new veterinary school is announced for the University of Calgary in 2004 with the aim of placing Alberta in the vanguard of animal-disease and food safety research.

WHAT GOES AROUND COMES AROUND

Neck in a Noose

The first white man hanged for murder in the North-West Territories is Jess Williams, on February 20, 1884.

Out You Creep

In 1888, Madame Nellie Webb gets rid of a drunken Mountie who is trying to force his way into her brothel, in Edmonton, by shooting him. No charges are laid against her.

Daylight Robbery

Three carloads of coal are stolen from a train in Nanton, February 5, 1907, during that particularly severe winter.

Prize Murderer

When murderer Wasyl Chobator is hanged on January 14, 1911, he is the first and only man ever hanged in Lethbridge.

Party Poopers

On New Year's Eve, 1912, police raid Lethbridge's red-light district for the first time.

Soap in your Mouth

Edmonton city council outlaws swearing in public in a new bylaw issued on November 24, 1922, after complaints about golfers swearing while playing on public courses.

Law Lady

Annie Jackson becomes the first female police officer in Canada. She serves with the Edmonton Police Department from 1912 until her marriage in 1918.

Heavenly Brew

Police in Lethbridge take an evangelist into custody, arrested for bootlegging on May 30, 1927, after a tip-off that his travelling church (a trailer towed behind his car) is actually a working distillery.

Give it Up, It's the Police!

The RCMP takes over policing responsibility for the province from the disbanded Alberta Provincial Police in 1930.

Last Murderer

In 1960, Robert Raymond Cook of Stettler becomes the last man hanged in Alberta after being convicted of murdering his parents. On November 14, he is led from his Fort Saskatchewan cell at midnight and pronounced dead at 12:18 AM.

Monkey See, Monkey Do

After a screening of the rap movie *CB4* in Edmonton on March 16, 1993, 100 youths run riot, attacking passersby at West Edmonton Mall and the downtown Eaton Centre Mall. The police use pepper spray and batons to bring the thugs under control.

Calgary Cop-ette

When Christine Silverberg is appointed Calgary's chief of police in 1995, she becomes the first female police chief in a major Canadian city.

A Chance to Reunite

A 1995 change in Alberta's adoption laws means it's now possible for parents who gave kids up, or children given up for adoption, to search for each other. In 2003 and 2004, 167 reunions are arranged through the Alberta Adoptions Registry.

Diminished Responsibility

Dorothy Joudris is acquitted on May 9, 1996, of attempted murder of her estranged husband, Calgary businessman Earl Joudrie. Her counsel successfully convinces the jury that when she shot him six times she was suffering from a mental disorder. Dorothy passed away at the Calgary Foothills Hospital in 2002, at the age of 66.

Copycat Killing

Inspired by the Littleton Colorado massacre eight days earlier, a 14-year-old boy murders fellow student Jason Lang with a .22-calibre rifle at the W.R. Myers High School in Taber on April 28.

Eco-Warrior's Revenge

Wiebo Ludwig bombs a gas-well near his ranch in 1998 because he believed it was causing deadly pollution near his ranch. He is convicted of the offence on April 19, 2000.

LIQUOR AND THE LAW

Drinks Ban

Prohibition is voted in by the Alberta Legislature in 1916. But anyone desperate for a drink is still legally allowed to brew their own or buy "medicinal" booze in pharmacies.

Good Job

The positive results of a "dry" province are less cases of domestic violence, an increase in bank savings and a reduction in crime overall. Unlike in the U.S., mobsters and acts of violence as a result of rum-running in Alberta are few and far between.

Alcoholic Hotspot

The Crowsnest Pass, the border crossing between BC and Alberta, becomes so flooded with bootleg booze making its way to Montana that local authorities send for cops in 1918 to put a cork in the trader's activities.

Rum-Runner's Revenge

The Pass is the scene of a car chase that ends with Constable Steve Lawson wounding liquor smuggler Steve Picariello. The rum-runner's dad, Emilio, seeks revenge for his son's injury and shoots the constable in the back in broad daylight. Florence Lassandro, Emilio's employee, is at his side at the shooting.

Accomplice or Innocent Bystander?

Emilio and Florence stand trial for murder in what has become known as Alberta's most famous murder case. They are both found guilty. The thought of a woman being hanged disgusts many Canadians, but the executions go ahead anyway on May 23, 1923. Florence, only 22 years old, maintains her innocence to the last. She is the last woman to be executed in Alberta. *Filumena*, an opera based on the story, is performed in Calgary in February 2003.

Florence Frees the Flow

Florence's murder trial adds fuel to Albertans' increasing disenchantment with eight years of Prohibition. A referendum is held in 1923, and the people of Alberta vote to lift Prohibition.

Provincially Licensed Liquor

Alberta's first government-owned liquor stores open for business in May 1924, a year after the executions.

Equal Drinkers

It isn't until 1957 that a ban on men and "unescorted" women drinking together in Alberta's bars is lifted.

Let the Good Times Roll

As a way to cut provincial debt by getting quick cash, Premier Ralph Klein privatizes all of Alberta's liquor stores, the first Canadian province to do so, in 1993. At the time the province has 304 retail outlets; by 2006, the number has grown to 1121 stores.

WORLD WAR I

Tarnished by the Same Brush

In 1916, a Calgary restaurant hires a couple of German-born employees, which proves too much for the local inhabitants to swallow. A mob of 500 tears the place apart.

A Woman's War

The 1917 Wartime Elections Act gives women serving in the armed forces the right to vote. It is also granted for ladies with relatives in the service. Conversely, citizens of "enemy alien" birth are disenfranchised.

Maybe a Good Day for Flying?

On April 12, 1918, the infamous "Red Baron," Manfred von Richthofen, shoots at Edmonton-born Wop May on the novice's very first combat flight, but misses. A lucky escape, because the Baron is already credited with shooting down 80 Allied aircraft. This proves to be the Baron's last sortie. He is killed by a bullet, possibly fired by Canadian pilot Arthur Brown. May goes on to become a flying ace himself. He shoots down 13 enemy aircraft and is awarded the Distinguished Flying Cross.

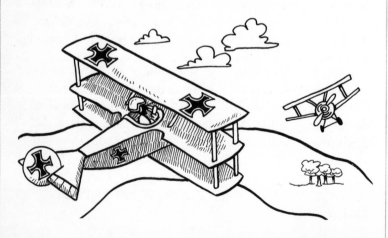

BETWEEN THE WARS

Yes, You May

After the war, on May 19, 1919, Wop May sets up the May Airplanes Company and flies his biplane, *The Edmonton*, on the first commercial flight in Western Canada. The plane can be seen today at the Reynolds Alberta Museum in Wetaskiwin.

Commemorate the Fallen

The inscription on Red Deer's cenotaph, unveiled on September 15, 1922, reads: *In proud and grateful remembrance of those who served in the Great War 1914–1918.*

Rallying the Troops

King George VI and Queen Elizabeth (later the "Queen Mum") visit Alberta on June 2, 1939, just before the outbreak of World War II—the first visit to Canada by a reigning sovereign. Portage Avenue in Edmonton is renamed Kingsway Avenue in his honour.

High Flyer

In 1936, Edmonton resident Punch Dickins receives the Order of the British Empire, OBE for his contribution to Canadian Aviation. He flies 73 missions in WWI and is the first bush pilot to fly over the Barren Lands in the eastern Arctic in 1928.

Magnets and Metals

A year later, in 1929, Punch flies the first airmail flight to the High Arctic—without a compass (because they don't work so close to the North Pole). Punch is also the first pilot to fly into Great Bear Lake, Northwest Territories, where Canada's first economically viable uranium discovery is made in 1930 by Gilbert Labine.

WORLD WAR II

Duty to Enlist

The first person to sign up for WWII military service in Canada is a Blood from the Fort Macleod reserve, Private Albert Mountain Horse. He meets his death at the Battle of Ypres in a cloud of poison gas. Between 1914 and 1919, 6000 Albertans die for their country in the Great War out of a total 39,000 who serve.

Signing Up

During World War II, more than one million Canadians serve in the country's army, navy and air force, including 50,000 women. In Alberta, more than half the province's adult population enlist.

DID YOU KNOW?

Over 12,000 First Nations, Métis and Inuit people fight for Canada in the First and Second World Wars and the Korean War of 1949–53.

Flight School

Because Canada's skies are big and free from enemy attack during WWII, the British Commonwealth government decide to stage a large part of its air training program in Canada. At its peak, 12 schools operate in southern Alberta out of a total of 231 across Canada, involving 10,840 aircraft and 131,000 pilots and ground staff.

"Enemy" Lock-Up

Lethbridge and Medicine Hat become Canada's largest WWII prisoner-of-war camps. Many people interned are civilians of Japanese descent who are banned from living in coastal areas in BC.

Belated Apologies and a Royal Affair

All is forgotten by 1967, when the Nikka Yuko Japanese Garden opens to celebrate Canada's Centennial. Japan's Prince and Princess Takamatsu lead a list of special guests.

Yanks North of the 49th

American soldiers "invade" Canada in 1942 to build the Alaska Highway and an oil pipeline.

Icy Killer

The National Research Council builds a secret warship made out of ice for the British government. The ship, started in 1942 at Patricia Lake, Jasper, is kept frozen during the summer of 1943 and eventually allowed to melt when the war was over.

Bittersweet

During WWII, Japanese Canadians from British Columbia are deemed untrustworthy and put to work in forced labour camps, growing sugar beet in Southern Alberta.

Balloon Blazes

Japan begins launching incendiary balloons in 1944, with the aim of causing forest fires in BC and Alberta. An unexploded balloon is found in Provost on February 7, 1945, by two young men. They accidentally detonate the fuse with a hot poker, which miraculously fails to ignite the explosive canister, and they escape with only minor injuries. Later that year, four other balloons fall on Alberta and ignite but do not cause much damage.

A Call to Arms

In 1943, a call goes out for all Canadians to turn in scrap metal. A curfew is also imposed, and in the village of Coronation, when Constable Venables rings the old firebell, it cracks and 150 kilograms of metal shower down on him. News of the mishap is broadcast around the world.

The Devil's Highway

In September 1999, the main highway between the City of Lethbridge and Helena in Montana is renamed the "First Special Service Force Memorial Highway" in honour of the route taken in 1942 by a group of Canadian volunteers to join forces with their American counterparts training at Fort Harrison. The unit, made up of 900 Canadian and 700 American commandos, is nicknamed The Devil's Brigade by the Germans because its soldiers blacken their faces for night raids.

Mission Accomplished

Only 113 of the 900 Canucks come back from the war. But the Brigade succeeds in every mission, wins five U.S. campaign stars and eight Canadian battle honours, and captures 30,000 prisoners between 1942 and 1944.

The War of No Return

During WWII, 3350 Albertan soldiers die of the 77,704 who went to the war.

Canada's Largest Mass Hanging

The execution of four German prisoners of war takes place at the Lethbridge Provincial Jail on December 18, 1946. Their crime is the murder of fellow prisoner Cpl. Karl Lehmann at the Medicine Hat POW camp in September 1944.

On Top of the World

Prime Minister Mackenzie King changes the name of Banff's Castle Mountain to Eisenhower Mountain, a thanks for U.S. help in WWII. Many Albertans are outraged, but it takes until 1979 to change the name back again to the original.

I Wanna Go Home

It takes a Lethbridge woman and her 13-year-old daughter nearly nine years to get back home to Alberta after travelling to Bulgaria in 1938. They get caught when WWII breaks out, then are stuck behind the Iron Curtain in 1945 when the post-war Communist government refuses to let them leave. After a diplomatic struggle they finally arrive home on December 9, 1947.

Military Might

The province's military heritage is sealed when CFB Cold Lake (on the border with Saskatchewan) is chosen as the site for a new Canadian Forces Base in 1952, because it has flat terrain, good drainage, gravel deposits and low population density. The base is operational by March 31, 1954. As an aside, the town of Cold Lake became Alberta's newest city on October 1, 2000.

DID YOU KNOW?

Cold Lake is a direct translation of the name given to the village by the Cree, based on an old legend. One night, many, many winters ago, a young man rows across the lake to visit his sweetheart. But a huge fish, the kinosoo, snaps his canoe in half, and the youth disappears into the chilly waters. The Cree people don't dare cross the lake for a long time afterwards and believe that the 2-metre-long trout that the first settlers routinely caught were direct descendants of the kinosoo.

ICE AND SNOW

Puck Power

Alberta's first recorded hockey game is a showdown in Calgary. The Town Boys beat the Tailors 4–1 in 1893. Edmonton's first hockey game is held on Christmas Day 1894 when the Edmonton Thistles beat Fort Saskatchewan 3–2.

Government on Ice

In 1906, Alberta's first legislative session opens at in Edmonton at the Thistle Curling Rink, then sits in the McKay Avenue School, because the legislative building hasn't been built yet.

Snow Sports
The Edmonton Ski Club is founded on December 19, 1911. Calgary's comes in 1920.

A Puck is Born
The Western Canada Hockey League is born in1921, with professional teams competing from Calgary, Edmonton, Regina and Saskatoon. The champions automatically qualify to play in the Stanley Cup finals.

King of the Ice

When the Edmonton Eskimos lose the Stanley Cup playoffs to the Ottawa Senators in 1923, it isn't for lack of effort from one of the players. In game two, King Clancy plays every position on the ice; he even goes in net when goalie Clint Benedict has to serve out a penalty.

National Pride in Alberta
It's 1950. The Edmonton Mercurys represent Canada at the World Hockey Championships in London, England, and win the gold medal.

Lady Champs Too

The Edmonton Flyers win the Women's Hockey League title in 1953.

Pros Take to the Ice

The Edmonton Oilers are the first professional team from Alberta to join the World Hockey Association in 1973. In 1974, the team moves to their current home, called the Northlands Coliseum until a name change in 2003 renames it Rexall Place.

Ski-Lift Luxury

In 1980, the Sunshine Village gondola begins winter operation, saving skiers a tough ride up the mountain.

Protégé Puck

Oiler Wayne Gretzky becomes the first teenage player in the NHL to score 50 goals in a season on April 2, 1980.

Champion of Champions

The Edmonton Oilers win the Stanley Cup five times between 1984 and 1990, including wins in 1985, 1987 and 1988.

On Fire

The Calgary Flames play their inaugural NHL game on June 24, 1980, and it takes them nine years to win their first Stanley Cup.

Gretzky Gone

Wayne Gretzky, known as the greatest-ever Canadian hockey player, is instrumental in the Edmonton Oilers' wins until 1988, when owner Peter Pocklington sells him to the Los Angeles Kings for $15 million USD. A tidy profit. Pocklington paid $850,000 for the then 17-year-old hockey phenomenon back in 1978.

Magic Gone

But Gretzky can't turn on the magic in LA. He helps the Kings go from 18th to 4th place in the NHL then has three off-years with the New York Rangers. He retires on April 16, 1999, at the age of 38, with 61 NHL records to his credit.

A Mighty Big Fall

In 1997, Peter Pocklington's halcyon days as owner of one of the world's most successful hockey teams are over when his financial troubles are revealed, and Alberta Treasury Branches seizes the Edmonton Oilers. Local investors pitch in to buy the team.

DID YOU KNOW?

During the Stanley Cup final series between the Bruins and the Oilers in 1988, game four is all square at 3–3 when the power in the Boston Garden arena suddenly goes out. It doesn't come back on either. So the game is replayed in Edmonton.

ALBERTANS WITH BALLS

Rivals at Rugger

On November 9, 1907, the Edmonton Rugby Foot-ball Club loses the first game it plays against the Calgary City Rugby Foot-ball Club 26–5.

Basketball Beauties

John Percy Page coaches the Edmonton Grads girls' basketball team through 522 games over 25 years. They lose only 20 matches, including national and international games against men's teams. They disband in 1940 because they've become so unbeatable, spectators get bored with them always winning.

Inventor's Accolade

James Naismith, the Canadian who invented basketball, describes the Grads as "the finest basketball team that ever stepped out on a floor."

From Bucking to Charging

The Calgary Broncs football team changes its name to the Calgary Stampeders on September 28, 1945.

Winning Stomp

The Calgary Stampeders win their first Grey Cup in 1948. A group of 300 Calgarians, led by the very boisterous Mayor Mackay, wear white cowboy hats to the game, and from then on any official guest of the city is given one. The hats became so reminiscent of the city that Calgary adopts the white cowboy hat as its civic symbol in 1959.

Calgary on the Rampage

The Calgary Stampeders win their first Grey Cup in 1992.

But Next Year...

The Edmonton Eskimos win the Grey Cup in 1993 for the first time since their record-breaking five wins in a row (1978–82). The Eskimos have won 13 Cups, the Stampeders 5. Only the Toronto Argonauts have won more Grey Cups than the Eskimos, with 15.

DID YOU  KNOW?

Today's CFL football team is called the Edmonton Eskimos. The first hockey team from the city to play in a Stanley Cup final, in 1908, was also called the Edmonton Eskimos.

The Road to Glory

The Oilers hockey victories, Edmonton Eskimo football wins and the success of the Grads basketball team mean Edmonton posts the moniker "City of Champions" on its highway signs.

REACHING HIGH

Peak and Valley

North America's first sporting mountaineer to die in a climbing accident is Philip Stanley Abbot in 1896. He fails to make it back down alive from the 3423-metre-high Mount Lefroy, which looks onto Lake Louise.

Peak Fitness

The first climbers to scale Mount Robson, the Canadian Rockies' highest peak, are Conrad Kain, Billy Foster and Albert MacCarthy who make the ascent in 1913.

On Top of the World

Sharon Wood, from Canmore, becomes the first Canadian and only the sixth woman ever to stand at the summit of Mount Everest in 1986. She is part of the second team from Canada to attempt the climb. On the previous Canadian attempt, in 1982, four climbers died.

HORSING AROUND

Toffs on Horseback

The first Western Canadian Polo Championship is held in Cowley in 1912. Many of Alberta's ranchers are English gentlemen who have brought their sports and pastimes with them.

First Past the Post

In 1986, 26-year-old Edmonton-born Gail Greenough becomes the first woman, the first Canadian, the first North American and the youngest person ever to win the World Show Jumping Championships. She is made a Member of the Order of Canada in 1990.

Thoroughbred Racetrack

Spruce Meadows is the world-class equine-centre-lovechild of ATCO owner Ron Southern and his wife Marg. Their dream is to create a quality show-jumping training facility in western Canada, and by 1976, the centre hosts its first tournament. A record attendance of 58,440 is reached on Sunday, September 7, 2003, during the Masters Tournament.

WINNING AT GAMES

Aboriginal Athlete

The only Albertan athlete at the 1912 Stockholm Olympics is Alex Decoteau, a Cree policeman from Edmonton. He runs the 5000 metres and finishes eighth.

Sports Stars

The Alberta Sports Hall of Fame and Museum opens for history buffs and sports fanatics in 1957. Since then 500 athletes have been honoured and inducted as members.

Let the Games Begin

Opened by Queen Elizabeth II, hosted for the first time in Canada and Alberta's first major international sporting event, Edmonton hosts the Commonwealth Games in 1978. At the closing ceremony on August 11, Canada has won 109 medals—45 gold, 31 silver and 33 bronze. Canadian swimmer Graham Smith, of Edmonton, is the first athlete to win six medals at a single Games.

Student Champions

Canada has its best-ever performance overall at the 1983 World University Games, coming in third behind the U.S. and USSR.

DID YOU  KNOW?

American network ABC pays a record $386 million for U.S. television rights to the 1988 Calgary Winter Olympics. CTV wins the rights to the Canadian feed.

Olympic Winners

Elizabeth Manley wins an unexpected figure-skating silver medal in the 1988 Calgary Winter Olympics. Other Canadian winners are Brian Orser, who won a silver for figure skating, Calgarian Karen Percy, two bronzes for Alpine skiing, and Robert McCall and Tracy Wilson, who win a bronze for ice dancing.

Olympic Competitors

In the 1988 Calgary Olympics, 1428 competitors from 57 nations compete in 46 events. Seven new events are included in the Winter Olympics this time–the men and women's super giant slalom, men's and women's alpine combined; team Nordic combined; team K120 ski jumping and the women's 5000-metre speed skating.

1988 Olympic Black and White

Debbi Thomas of the U.S. goes down in history as the first black winner of a Winter Olympic gold. She wins bronze in women's figure skating.

Golden Boy

Kurt Browning wins his first of four Men's World Figure Skating Championships on March 16, 1989.

Breaking Down Barriers

Sergei Priakin becomes the first Soviet player allowed to play in North America by the Soviet Ice Hockey Federation when he is signed by the Calgary Flames on March 29, 1989.

No Canadian Gold

Edmonton hosts the World Figure Skating Championships, March 25, 1996. Russians win the ice dance and pairs gold medals; the U.S. takes the individual ladies' and men's.

Broadcasting Biceps

Stu Hart, an amateur-champ-turned-promoter, started Stampede Wrestling in Calgary. By the late 1970s and 1980s, Friday night crowds pack his arena, and the shows are watched around the world on TV the next afternoon.

Baring it All

Salt Lake City Olympic cross-country skiing gold medal winner Beckie Scott poses nude in a calendar called "Nordic Nudes" in 2001 to help raise money for the Canadian Women's Nordic ski team.

Lifelong Dream Achiever

After winning gold in the women's 500-metre speed skating on February 14, 2002, at the Salt Lake City Olympic Games, Calgary resident Catriona Le May Doan retires from the sport to have a baby.

The Alchemy of Honesty

Vermilion native Beckie Scott gets a pleasant surprise after winning bronze in the cross-country skiing event at Salt Lake Olympics on February 15, 2002. Her medal is later upgraded to silver, because the two Russians who placed first and second are found to be under the influence of performance-enhancing drugs. Two years later, after an exhausting battle led by the Canadian Olympic Committee, the silver is upgraded to gold.

ENERGETIC ALBERTA

Smarts Ahead of Their Time

The Natives already know about oil back in 1719. A Cree called Swan takes a sample of Athabasca tar sands to the Hudson's Bay Company. They think it's useless.

The First Oil Man

Peter Pond, a fur trader, is the white first man to see the oil-sands. He witnesses a Native waterproofing his canoe in 1778 with tar sands found in the Athabasca river.

Old and New

Alberta's three oilsands deposits—Athabasca, Cold Lake and Peace River—cover 77,000 km^2 and together contain two-thirds of the world's bitumen.

Black as Night

Explorer and fur trader Peter Fiddler discovers Alberta's coal in 1792.

A Salty Taste in the Mouth

Alfred von Hammerstein, a German immigrant, is one of the first men to investigate the oilsands in 1906. The only thing to come of his drilling, however, is a discovery of salt, and he sets up the Alberta Salt Company in the 1920s instead.

Busting to Get Out

George Mercer Dawson, a Boundary Commission employee, is the first man to note oil seepage in the Waterton Lakes area in August 1874.

Watery End

Nicholas Sheran establishes Alberta's first commercial coal mine in 1874 in a place called Coalbanks, known today as the city of Lethbridge. Eight years later, he drowns in the South Saskatchewan River.

Black as Night

Alberta's coal production goes up from 240,000 tonnes in 1897 to 3 million tonnes in 1910 and 4 million tonnes by 1913.

Lucky Strike

On December 12, 1883, CPR crews digging for water near Medicine Hat get an early Christmas present and find natural gas instead. The gas catches fire and burns the derrick!

It's All Mine

Mr. A.P. Patrick files the first petroleum claim in 1889 for a strike in Waterton.

There She Blows

The Rocky Mountain Development Company drill the first well in Western Canada to produce oil. The oil strike occurs at a depth of 310 metres, on September 21, 1902, at the Waterton National Park.

Stinker Town

That same year Medicine Hat establishes the first municipally-owned gas system in Canada. You could smell it, and so could Rudyard Kipling when he visits in 1907 and delivers his famous line describing the town as having "all hell for a basement."

That's a Big Slide

In 1903, it takes just 90 seconds for an estimated 14,100 m³ of rock to cascade down Turtle Mountain in the Crowsnest Pass, burying part of the village and the Frank Mine below. Seventy-six people die in the "Frank Slide," as it becomes known, in Canada's worst natural disaster.

Lucky and Not So Lucky

The force of the slide throws rocks more than a kilometre, while shards spear and kill people in their beds. Marion Leitch, only 15 months old, is sucked through a hole in the roof of her home. Luckily she lands in a bale of hay. Her two sisters also escape unharmed, but her parents and four brothers die.

The Right to Fight

Lethbridge miners wage a nine-month strike in 1906 when their employer refuses to recognize their union, The United Mine Workers of Alberta.

Water Power

Alberta's first hydro-electric power plant is built in 1911 at Horseshoe Falls.

Pure Black Gold

The oil that spews from 1914 Dingman well discovery in the Turner Valley is so pure that the primitive cars of that day can be filled up on the spot. The oilfield's gas flares are so bright Calgary is bathed in light. Just over 20 years later, there are 294 wells in operation in the area, Alberta's first oil boom.

Canada's Worst Mining Disaster

An explosion at the Hillcrest Mine in the Crowsnest Pass at 9:30 AM, June 19, 1914, kills 189 people. One hundred and thirty wives lose their husbands, and more than 400 children their fathers. The miners' bodies are buried in mass graves, later enclosed by a picket fence, near the rubble left by the earlier Frank Slide.

Lucrative Washing Machine
Alberta's first oil refinery opens in Calgary in 1923.

Hands Off Our Energy!

In 1930, Premier Brownlee wrests jurisdiction over the province's natural resources from the federal government in the Natural Resources Transfer Act. Modern Albertans are very, very grateful.

Experimental Extraction
Bituminous Sands Permit No. 1 is granted to Max Ball and the Canadian Northern Oil Company, based in Fort McMurray in 1930.

Father of Oil Industry Communications

Nickle's Daily Oil Bulletin, a leading source of energy information today, starts life in 1937 as a one-page typewritten journal produced by Calgary radio reporter Carl Nickle.

11th Hour Belly-Up
In 1936, Alberta's economy is in disastrous shape during the Depression. The Social Credit Government defaults on its debts but is saved by another monumental strike of crude oil in the Turner Valley.

Big Splash
On a farm belonging to Mike Turta, near Leduc, a massive oil strike on February 3, 1947, transforms Alberta's economy, fuelling $100 billion worth of provincial gross domestic product over the next 50 years.

Nearly Didn't Happen

The Leduc bonanza, drilled by Vern Hunter, is Imperial Oil's 134th attempt in Western Canada. The previous 133 had turned up dry, and exploration is just about to be abandoned. Hunter led the teams responsible for many of these failures so consequently earns the nickname "Dryhole." After the strike, the creators of this moniker are no doubt gushing to apologize.

Up in Smoke

Alberta's largest coal dock at Coronation burns to the ground on August 3, 1939. The fire allegedly starts at the top of the heap from spontaneous combustion and consumes 200 tonnes of coal.

Alberta's First Pipeline

Designed to carry oil from Alberta to Lakehead, Thunder Bay, Ontario, construction starts on the $95-million Interprovincial Pipeline on April 30, 1950. The first barrel of oil arrives on April 24, 1952.

Wells Like Rabbits

By 1953, 4272 wells are drilling in the province under the watchful eyes of Texan advisors on how to drill and distribute black gold.

And Then There Were Trees

The first pulp mill in the province starts chopping in 1957.

Pay Dirt

Exploration of the oilsands begins in earnest in 1964 with various projects run by Great Canadian Oilsands Ltd. (now Suncor). The first commercial tar sands separation plant in Fort McMurray starts life in 1967.

Go, Oilers, Go
Great Canadian Oilsands delivers the first barrel of oil from the Athabasca tar sands in 1967.

Demand Up, Supply Down

In 1974, oil prices rise sharply because of the Arab oil boycott, spurring a period of crazy oil exploration in Western Canada. The "oilpatch" is headquartered in Calgary and grows rapidly— the city's population expands from 325,000 in 1974 to 650,000 by the early 1980s.

It IS a Bird!

The frenzy of downtown construction leads locals to declare the "provincial bird of Calgary" is a construction crane! So many old buildings are replaced the locals joke that any building pre-dating the 1974–1980 oil boom is a candidate for being declared a heritage site.

Nationalized Interest

On July 30, 1975, Ottawa sets up Petro-Canada, based in Calgary, as a Crown Corporation to exert Canadian influence in the oil industry and exploit national energy resources worldwide.

Waiting in the Wings
Syncrude becomes the second biggest player in Alberta when it produces its first barrel of oil refined from the Athabasca tar sands in 1978.

Taxing Times

Ottawa grabs an increasing share of Alberta's oil revenues and its wrath under the National Energy Program introduced by Prime Minister Trudeau in 1980. The program runs until 1985, and its demise heralds a period of friendship building between Alberta and Ottawa.

Rock Bottom

In 1986, oil bottoms out at its lowest-ever relative price. Sixty-five thousand Albertans end up unemployed, the worst economic crisis since the Great Depression of the 1930s.

A Spark in the Wind
Calgary's VisionQuest Windelectric Inc. install Alberta's first wind turbine connected to an electricity grid in 1983. The company also creates Canada's first wind farm at Cambridge Bay, Nanavut, in 1993.

Bottom of the League

In global wind power production Canada is at the bottom of the scale in the world's countries—Ottawa produces 215 megawatts and Alberta, with 93 megawatts, most of the rest. Germany is the leading producer worldwide with 9500 megawatts. Put into perspective, 30 million megawatt hours of electricity per year meet the electricity needs of nearly four million homes.

A History of the Future for Alberta?
According to Environment Canada, in 2003, of the country's 12 worst polluters, three Alberta companies make up the ranks: Syncrude at number seven, TransAlta at number eight and EnCana at number 12. Ontario's Inco is number one, followed by Alcan in Québec and Nova Scotia Power.

Cleaning Up Our Act

In 2003, Alberta produces 25 percent of Canada's air pollution with only 10 percent of the country's population, surpassing Ontario for the first time.

MUSICAL MILESTONES

The First Grand

Alberta's first grand piano is brought to the province by Sir James Lougheed and housed in his palatial Calgary mansion called Beaulieu, built in 1891. Lougheed, a businessman and lawyer, becomes one of the founders of the Law Society of Alberta, a Senator, Privy Councillor, and member of the Order of St. Michael and St. George. He is grandfather to Peter Lougheed, the provincial premier who holds power from 1971 to 1985.

Twinkle Little Star

In 1909, at the age of 12, Calgarian Gladys McKelvie is the first Canadian to win a three-year scholarship to the Royal Academy of Music in London, England.

Musical Metamorphosis

The Calgary Symphony Orchestra debuts at the Sherman Grand Theatre before an audience of over 700 people on January 27, 1913. It disbands at the outbreak of World War I and is reborn in 1949 only to be absorbed six years later by the Calgary Philharmonic Orchestra in 1955.

It Doesn't Have to be Big to be Brilliant

Lethbridge's Symphony Orchestra has been performing in the city since 1960.

Dulcet Export

Calgary opera singer Norma Piper receives standing ovations and much acclaim on her concert tour of Italy in 1929.

Wilf Who?

In 1933, Calgary's Wilf Carter is the man responsible for the world's first recording of an "echo" yodel, a three-in-one call he practised in the Rocky Mountains and that few, if any, other singers can emulate. Wilf ends World War II era as the most popular country music star in Canada.

Dulcet Tones
The Edmonton Symphony Orchestra plays its first concert in 1952, the same year Elizabeth II is crowned "Elizabeth the Second, by the Grace of God, of the United Kingdom, Canada and Her other Realms and Territories Queen, Head of the Commonwealth, Defender of the Faith."

Baby Boomers Songs
Janis Joplin plays to a sold-out crowd in Calgary in 1970.

A Jubilee Hit
In August 1971, the English rock band Procol Harum records a live album at the city's Jubilee Auditorium in collaboration with the Edmonton Symphony Orchestra. One of the songs, *Conquistador,* is released a year later and becomes a top 10 hit.

Folk Born
Alberta's 75th birthday, in 1980, means cash for commemorative events. So the government forks out $120,000 for a caravan of folk singers to tour the province in a show called the Travelling Folk Festival and Goodtime Medicine Show. After the tour, some of the artists play the first Edmonton Folk Music Festival, using sound equipment borrowed from the bus.

Any Volunteers
The Folk Fest's founder Don Whelan, an Edmonton concert promoter, pulls it off thanks to 300 volunteers who give their time in exchange for entrance tickets. Todayn about 500 volunteers help out each year.

Big Songs
Edmonton's Folk Festival is the largest in Canada. Calgary's comes in fourth, after second place Winnipeg and Vancouver in third.

Little Fest
There are arts festivals today in the province's smaller communities including Drumheller, Okotoks, Lesser Slave Lake, Sylvan Lake and Fort Macleod. They are all kick-started in the mid-1970s by support for the arts spearheaded by Premier Peter Lougheed.

Let Down
In July 1988, 11,000 fans in Calgary and Edmonton get refunds after British rock singer Sting cancels his concerts.

Stones Sell Out

Tickets to the 1997 Rolling Stones concerts at Commonwealth Stadium sell out in 49 minutes.

Shock Rocker Banned from Town

A concert by Marilyn Manson is called off in Calgary on July 16, 1997, after the owner of the Max Bell Arena bows to pressure from church groups to stop the show going ahead. A judge refuses to grant an injunction sought by the artist to force the owner into letting the concert go ahead.

Out of the Mouths of Babes

In response to the plight of children affected by the December 26, 2004, tsunami in the Indian Ocean, 10-year-old Aysha Wills has a brainwave. Her idea is to put on a small recital with the Edmonton Symphony Orchestra to raise funds for the global aid effort. The concept blossoms into an enormous benefit concert and silent auction called Higher Ground on February 4, 2005, at the Frances Winspear Centre for Music in Edmonton. The event raises $600,000 and Aysha is named Global TV's Woman of Vision for March 2005.

Singing Before He Could Speak

Eighteen-year-old Kalan Porter, winner of *Canadian Idol 2004, Season 2*, is born on the Sundance Buffalo Ranch near Irvine, southeast of Medicine Hat. He wins the show with 3.6 million votes, beating Karan and Theresa Sokyrka of Saskatoon. According to his mother, Kalan was able to hum parts of Brahm's *Lullaby* at 18 months.

Tribute to Musical Genius

In 2006, the Banff Centre for the Arts celebrates the 250th anniversary of Mozart's birth with a performance of *The Magic Flute*.

STAGE AND SCREEN

Junior Top Hat

Twelve-year-old Fred Astaire makes his stage debut at the Sherman Theatre, Calgary, in 1912.

Another Star Visitor

At 70 years of age, the famous French actress Sarah Bernhard could still stun audiences. She did so by reciting the tragedy *Lucretia Borgia* in French at Calgary's Sherman Grand Theatre on January 14, 1913. At the time the theatre has the largest stage anywhere in Canada.

The Show Still Goes On

Bashaw, northeast of Red Deer, is home to western Canada's only remaining "Boomtown" theatre, the Majestic, built in 1915. The building, a rural wooden frame show-house, has staged magic lantern shows, local theatre productions, silent movies, early "talkies" and even served, temporarily, as Bashaw's first Catholic Church.

DID YOU KNOW?

"Boomtown" is the name given to towns that spring up overnight all over North America as soon as railways arrive. The phenomenon spawns its own particular style of architecture characterized by a grandly designed façade, covering a humble building behind it. The best examples still survive on the "Boomtown Trail" that connects Camrose (50 kilometres south of Edmonton) to Strathmore (40 kilometres east of Calgary).

First Flick

In 1961, *Wings of Chance* becomes the first movie made in
Alberta by Albertans. It is produced by Larry Matanksi.

Tippytoes and Tights

The Alberta Ballet is founded by Ruth Carse in 1966, the same
year that saw the first-ever live colour television broadcast, soc-
cer's World Cup Final when England beat West Germany 4–2.

A Case for Carse

Ruth Carse leaves Alberta at the age of 21 to study in Toronto
because there were no dance facilities in the province. Her dad
bets her $100 she'll be back within a month. After a successful
career in the U.S. and Europe, she comes home 17 years later,
but it is only a torn Achilles tendon that forces the return.
Carse founds the Alberta Ballet School in 1971.

Men in Tights in Calgary

Footlights at the city's first regional theatre are lit up in 1968
when Theatre Calgary starts life in a converted tractor barn.

Flowers Bloom in the Desert

Joe Shoctor launches Edmonton's Citadel Theatre from an old
Salvation Army citadel in 1965, which he converts into a 277-
seat venue at a cost of $250,000. *Who's Afraid of Virginia Wolfe?*
is the first play staged there. The restaurant in the theatre's basement is run by Tommy Banks, who goes on to become one of
Canada's most famous variety TV hosts, big-band conductors
and Liberal senators.

Travelling Theatre

Between 1968 and 1985, the Citadel on Wheels and Wings travels round the province bringing first-class theatre to 325 communities. Today 500 performances a year are staged in the new building, which opened in 1976. This includes more world premieres than any other Canadian theatre.

DID YOU  KNOW?

In 1960, Joe Shoctor becomes the youngest lawyer in Canada to become a QC (Queen's Counsel) at 38 years of age. He is also one of the founders of the Edmonton Eskimo Football Club and becomes instrumental in taking the team all the way to the CFL.

Ol' Rabbit

Theatre Calgary is that city's oldest independent company, established in 1968. The city's most well-known company is One Yellow Rabbit, started in 1982, known as a producer of avant-garde and local original works.

Theatre on the Edge

Edmonton's Fringe Theatre Festival takes its first step into the footlights in 1982 and is now the biggest theatrical event in North America. Worldwide, it is rivalled only by the Fringe in Edinburgh, Scotland. Half a million visitors attend more than 150 artistic endeavours from plays to poetry.

Stepping Out

The Canadian Film and Television Association holds its annual meeting in Edmonton, in 1975, the first time ever away from home base Toronto.

Stars in Their Eyes

The Alberta Motion Picture Industry Association is established by five production companies in 1973 to promote the movie industry. Today the organization lobbies government, provides grants and training and holds an annual awards ceremony, which in 2006 has a record number of 640 entries.

THE PRINTED WORD

Make 'em Laugh

In 1902, Robert C. Edwards puts Calgary on the map as editor of the *Calgary Eye Opener,* a newspaper with a readership that spans the globe. The paper, an irreverent satirical news commentary and gossip column, sells around 35,000 copies, the highest circulation of any paper published west of Winnipeg.

Double Standards

Editor Edwards loves to drink and proclaims the beauty of Calgary is caused by the fact it "is picturesquely situated so as to be within easy reach of the brewery, with streets revolving in eccentric orbits around a couple of dozen large bars." Surprisingly, Edwards supported Prohibition. "Our frank opinion is that the complete abolition of strong drink would solve the problem of the world's happiness," joked his newspaper.

Women Who Write

Katherine Hughes joins the staff of the *Edmonton Bulletin* in 1906 and becomes the first female journalist in Alberta. She also becomes the province's first archivist.

Elementary, My Dear Watson

Sherlock Holmes author Arthur Conan Doyle visits Jasper Park on June 24, 1923, as a guest of Richard P. Gough, one of the directors of Canadian National Railways.

Freedom of the Press

The *Edmonton Journal,* the *Calgary Herald* and 94 other newspapers in the province wage a fierce battle against the Social Credit Government's Accurate News and Information Act, which attempts to force newspapers to divulge their sources and to run government supplied articles. The Supreme Court of Canada strikes down the law, and the newspapers win a Pulitzer Prize for their trouble in 1938.

The Fifth Estate

The *Edmonton Journal* becomes an advocate again in 1979, when its fiery publisher Patrick O'Callaghan fights back after a federal raid on his offices that result in "seizing files for unexplained reasons." It may have something to do with O'Callaghan's personal crusade against the City's councillors who voted themselves a 60-percent pay increase behind closed doors. Callaghan's fight against the document seizure goes all the way to the Supreme Court. He becomes the first Canadian to use the Charter of Rights and Freedoms (1982) to ensure freedom of the press.

A Library of Books

Edmonton-born Mel Hurtig opens one of the city's first bookstores in 1956, which grows into the largest of its kind in Canada at 650 m². As a publisher, Hurtig Books prints landmark titles such as *The Canadian Encyclopedia*. Produced at a cost of $12 million, the encyclopedia is claimed by some to be the greatest accomplishment in the history of Canadian publishing. Hurtig sells his company to McClelland and Stewart in 1991.

Booming Arts

By the late 1970s, Alberta has the second largest publishing industry in Canada with over 30 companies and the nation's second largest film industry.

Publishing Profits Plummet

By 2006, prospects for publishing prove pitiful because the province provides poor subsidies compared to the grants made in other provinces. Six major publishing houses in Alberta are sold to out-of-province interests in the five-year period from 2001 to 2006.

Surviving without Subsidies

Windspeaker, a magazine published by the Aboriginal Multimedia society of Alberta, is one of only two (out of 11) aboriginal publications across Canada to survive the abolition of the Federal government's Native Communications Program in 1990. The paper becomes legendary for its outspoken commentaries, goes national and now turns in a healthy profit that helps fund four other aboriginal publications and a radio station.

Wizards Suffered, Too

In 2003, Albertan academics Andrew Gow and Lara Apps publish *Male Witches in Early Modern Europe*, which claims that male witches suffered just as much as females during Europe's notorious witch trials. The authors suggest that a quarter of the estimated 60,000 witches executed between 1450 and 1750 were men.

RADIO AND TELEVISION

Free Radio

When Radio CFAC hits the airwaves on August 19, 1922, it goes down in history as Calgary's first radio station as well as the first privately owned station transmitting between Vancouver and Winnipeg. The station's first broadcast features the Salvation Army band in concert.

Public Service

CKUA radio, Canada's oldest public broadcaster, is first licensed as the station of the University of Alberta in 1927.

The West Becomes Bilingue

The French arm of the CBC, La Société Radio-Canada, extends its French programming to listeners as far west as Calgary and Edmonton on October 26, 1950.

Birth of Broadcasting

In 1954, Alberta's first television station, CHCT-TV, starts broadcasting in Calgary, followed by CFRN in Edmonton.

TV Brains

Canada's first on-air educational TV station, ACCESS, starts broadcasting from Edmonton in 1970.

Piped Entertainment

Shaw Communications land the first cable television licence from the newly created Canadian Radio-Television and Communications Commission (CRTC), to cablecast in Edmonton in 1968. Today the company serves the whole province.

Selling Telly

The Banff International Festival of Films for Television is first held in 1979 and has become one of the world's most important market places for TV producers to sell product to broadcasters.

ALBERTA'S ARTS ADVANTAGE

Mountain Arts

Banff Summer School for the Arts opens in 1933. Today's Banff Centre for the Arts attracts visitors the world over in workshops and conference on writing, ballet, dance, sculpture, opera, electronic media. You name it, there's a workshop for it.

Canuck Collector

In 1954, millionaire oilman Eric Harvie sets up the Glenbow Foundation to house his artworks and treasures depicting the West's history. He donates the collection to Albertans in 1976 as part of the newly founded Glenbow Museum—the most extensive collection of Canadiana in the nation. There are enough documents, photographs and maps housed in the library's archives to top 26 Calgary Towers, which stands 190 meters tall.

Oil Rush Pushes Culture

In 1957, flush with oil profits, Alberta spends more per person on culture and social services than any other province in the country.

The Gold Rush Reborn

In 1962, Edmonton launches the Klondike Days exhibition so everyone could dress up in turn of the century costumes, eat drink and be merry. The name is changed to Capital Ex in 2005, but no one really knows why or what will be commemorated now.

Golden Age of the Arts

From 1971 to 1985, the premier of Alberta, Peter Lougheed, under the influence of his wife Jeanne, becomes Alberta's most influential patron of the arts. Jeanne fund-raises, sits on arts boards and attends every opening night possible. Together, the couple creates a golden age that transforms culture in Alberta from agriculture to the arts. Lougheed's government establishes the Alberta Heritage Fund in 1976, siphoning off a portion of oil revenues into savings, investments and long-term cultural investment.

DID YOU  KNOW?

Peter Lougheed has a provincial park named after him in Kananaskis Country.

Foreign Representative

In 1971, Horst Schmid becomes the first post-WWII immigrant elected to Alberta's Legislature. Lougheed appoints him minister of culture, youth and recreation in the cabinet.

Artistic Foothold

The Alberta Foundation for the Arts starts life in 1972. Funding for it comes from the government, which matches privately raised funds dollar for dollar (up to 25 percent of cost) for many productions.

A Right Royal Row

Plans to redecorate Government House in case Elizabeth II decides to visit the building while in Edmonton for the 1978 Commonwealth Games turn into a massive brawl between artists and government. Artists are first selected, then later rejected, on the grounds their works are too abstract and unfit for Her Majesty. After the threat of a class action lawsuit, the government backs down, and the art now hangs in Government House and other public buildings.

From Pies to Poetry

Until 1974, much of the province's arts and culture is based around farming communities and the 4-H rural youth clubs. But people want more than fruit pies and line dancing, so Edmonton leads the way and the rest of Alberta follows.

Food Fest

The three-day cultural festival of Edmonton Heritage Festival bills itself as the World's Largest Celebration of Cultural Diversity and Ethnic Harmony. Annually, 70 cultures pitch 50 pavilions in Hawrelak Park, Edmonton. The festival was launched in 1974.

Millennium Memoriam

At 97 years of age, Grant MacEwan dies in the year 2000. He had become Alberta's most eminent historian as well as serving as a university dean, alderman, MLA, mayor, leader of the Alberta Liberal Party, lieutentant-governor, scientist, and environmentalist and being named a member of the Order of Canada. He wrote 56 books, 3000 newspaper columns, 5000 speeches and made 1000 broadcasts. He has a library, a community college, a school, a neighbourhood and 24 streets named after him.

FROM BRIDGES TO BIO-TECH

First Canadian Flight

In 1907, the Underwood Brothers from Stettler build Canada's first runway in a bid to launch a flying machine they hoped would win a contest to achieve the first flight in the British Empire. They can't afford a motor, so settle on a kite. It works. The contraption soars in front of a stunned audience of farmers for 15 minutes, piloted by the youngest brother, but because it has no engine, it is disqualified from competition.

The Longest Chugging of All

Completed in 1909, the Lethbridge Viaduct, locally known as the High Level Bridge, is the longest railway bridge of its kind in the world.

Building Bridges

The first train crosses the High Level Bridge in Edmonton on June 2, 1913. The bridge is 750 metres long and about 50 metres above the North Saskatchewan River. The Low Level Bridge is the first Edmonton-area bridge, opening in 1900.

Developing the Future

The Alberta Research Council (ARC) is established in 1921, when the province is 16 years old with a population of 588,000. ARC's goal is to quantify the province's mineral resources, with a particular focus on bitumen deposits, and then to exploit them commercially. Today the organization also conducts research and business development in the life sciences, agriculture, forestry and manufacturing industries.

University of Newness

More than 130 unique technologies have patents issued to the University of Alberta. One of the earliest patents is Karl Clark's 1929 invention of Bituminous Sand Processing, now known as oilsands processing. The method patents a hot water and caustic soda mixture that is added to the oilsands under high temperatures using steam. In this way the solid sand and liquid bitumen separate, rendering the latter available for refining.

Honourable Troughs

In 1936, Charles Noble, a farmer from Lethbridge, develops the Noble Blade, an innovative plough that slices through weeds under the sod but leaves topcover above ground to prevent the soil from being blown away. By 1951, over $1 million worth of blades are sold annually. Noble dies in 1957.

Flying Snowmobiles

On April 8, 1941, Albertan Wilfred Leigh Brintnell patents a ski mechanism for landing aircraft in snow.

Hoe Hoe a Lady Inventor

There weren't many women getting patents in 1940s Alberta, but Tofield farmer Frances Kallal gets one in 1943. Tired of having to carry a hoe and a rake through all the rows of her large garden, she decides to put the two together, and hey presto, a hoe rake. The tool never goes into mass production but Kallal's daughter Margaret Dickson still uses her mother's original, 60 years later.

Preventative Medicine

A polio vaccine becomes widely available to Albertans after successful trials conducted in 1959 by the Connaught Medical Research Laboratories, University of Toronto, on 1.8 million children in Alberta, Saskatchewan and Manitoba.

Homes on Wheels

Calgary's Don Southern creates the mobile home unit commonly known as the ATCO trailer in 1946. He becomes the largest mobile home dealer in western Canada, selling $1million worth a year by the early 1950s. Don's son, Ron, goes on to become chairman of the board at ATCO and it grows into a multinational empire of power generation, electricity, gas, pipelines and defence businesses.

Knights in Shining Armour...On Wheels

In 1975, ATCO provides emergency housing in Darwin, Northern Australia, after destruction caused by Cyclone Tracy on Christmas Day, 1974.

Strike!

Bruno Scherzinger of Calgary scores a big hit in 1956 with a patent for a successful bowling alley pin-resetting machine.

Light Me Up and Show Me

On March 21, 1967, Harvey C. Nesbitt patents his "oil dipstick illuminator," a gadget that lights up according to the volume of oil inside a container. The device goes into mass production July 22.

Shoot the Blond

Keith R. Johnson of Edmonton patents a hairdresser's gun to dispense hair dye in 1969.

Gadget Geek

Calgary lawyer Jacob Bell Barron's first invention is a 1927 stereopticon (a projector or "magic lantern" having two lenses to create a three-dimensional picture) for use in movie theatres. Next comes a distinctive tobacco pipe in 1934 where the bowl rests on a perforated metal disc to prevent tobacco clogging up the airway. But his greatest success is the 1947 Barron Coin Roller that wraps coins in paper.

Finesse in Forestry

In 1984, Reg Isley launches his Grand Prairie equipment manu-facturing company and his revolutionary RotoSaw, "a mechanical harvesting head that cuts trees faster and with less fibre damage than other logging mechanisms." Isley has 32 patents under his belt that have helped put Alberta's forestry industry on the inter-national map.

Natural Medicine in Bottles

Since 1990, bio-tech pioneers, CV Technologies from Edmonton, has become a world leader in developing standard-ization tools to analyze natural-health products and isolate their active ingredients in an effort to "create a new paradigm of pre-ventative medicine." The process is refined during the develop-ment phase of the company's incredibly successful nutraceutical COLD-fX, made with the health-boosting attributes of American ginseng. COLD-fX is Canada's number one selling cold remedy endorsed by people like Don Cherry, Olympian speed skater Clara Hughes, and Kevin Lowe, general manager of the Edmonton Oilers.

Big Time Dot.com Bonanza

An Alberta farmer from Two Hills, Victor Chrapko sells his two-year-old company DocSpace for $800 million in 1999. The company provides an Internet site where people can share huge files containing things like photos and blueprints safely and securely.

WOMEN GET INVOLVED

No Husband? Time to Vote!

In 1885, unmarried women property owners living in the area now known as Alberta gain the right to vote and hold office in school matters.

Suffering Suffragettes

On October 9, 1914, Nellie McClung dumps a petition at the door of the Alberta Legislature, demanding the right to vote for women. Premier Sifton's response is to ask if Nellie and her supporters had washed the dishes before having the audacity to come and petition him.

X Marks the Spot

In 1916, women are granted the right to vote in provincial elections and to run for office. The Equal Suffrage Act also gives women "absolute equality" with men in provincial, municipal and school affairs. It thus permits women to vote and run for office in all Alberta-based elections. And the next general federal election in 1918 sees them allowed to vote there, too.

Parliamentary Equal

Alberta's Louise McKinney and Roberta MacAdams become the first women elected to a provincial legislature in the British Empire, in 1917.

Yes, Ma'am

When Emily Murphy is appointed a police magistrate on January 1, 1916, she becomes the first female judge in the British Commonwealth.

Big Year for the Ladies

The year 1921 marked many major achievements for women in politics. Irene Parlby is elected to the Alberta Legislature and becomes the first woman cabinet minister in Alberta and the second woman cabinet minister in the British Empire.

Alberta's Famous Five

Henrietta Muir Edwards, Louise McKinney, Emily Murphy, Irene Parlby and Nellie McClung are remembered as the women who made the most lasting contribution to political change in 20th-century Canada. The women became known as the "Famous Five" and win through in the "Person's Case." In 1929, women are legally recognized as persons with equal rights to men and therefore eligible to hold any political position.

Famous Fifty

The 75th anniversary of the Person's Case is commemorated in 2004. The "Famous Five" now appear on a new $50 bill. A monument to the women is also unveiled at Olympic Plaza in Calgary in 1999 and another on Parliament Hill in Ottawa in 2000.

STRANGE BEDFELLOWS

The Reds Are Coming

The town of Blairmore, in the Crowsnest Pass, declares itself
Canada's first Communist town in 1931, under Mayor Bill
Knight, in response to the Great Depression.

Power to the People

Canada's first major democratic socialist movement is established
in Calgary on August 1, 1932. It is called the Co-operative
Commonwealth Federation and its first leader is J.S. Woodsworth.
The party's social concepts developed into government programs
that are today deemed fundamental to Canadian society, such as
social assistance and public health insurance. The CCF is a pre-
cursor to the New Democratic Party.

Métis Freedom Fighters

Mirroring demands made by Métis leaders Riel and Gabriel
Dumont in wanting a land base and political autonomy, the
L'Association des Métis d'Alberta et des Territories du Nord-
Ouest holds its first convention in St. Albert on November 28,
1932. Autonomy is not granted, but the Alberta government's
Métis Betterment Act of 1938 sets aside 12 settlements for the
Nation in various parts of Alberta.

Racists Inc.

The Alberta government sanctions a request from the Klu Klux
Klan to incorporate as a business and set up their provincial
head office in Edmonton, during the early 1930s.

Good Loser

Fred Speed is the most consistent loser in Alberta politics. In
1934, he fails in his sixth and final attempt to get elected mayor
of Edmonton.

Apathetic or Happy with Alberta's Political Dynasties?

Albertans have the strange habit of creating political dynasties—keeping a party in power for a long, long time.

- ☛ Three Liberal premiers last 16 years from 1905 to 1921
- ☛ Three UFA premiers last 14 years from 1921 to 1935
- ☛ Three Social Credit premiers last 36 years from 1935 to 1971
- ☛ Three Conservative premiers last 35 years from 1971 and still going strong

Cash Crashes

In 1936, in the middle of the Great Depression, the Social Credit government of Alberta defaults on over $3 million worth of bonds.

That Cash Is a Joke!

In 1937, Premier Aberhart introduces Alberta Prosperity Certificates, a new currency, but most businesses refuse to accept it and so do his own Cabinet Ministers as part of their salary. The certificates are withdrawn, and the idea declared bankrupt.

The First Aboriginal Senator

Three years before Treaty Indians are given the right to vote in federal elections, Albertan James Gladstone becomes the first Aboriginal appointed to the Senate in 1958.

A Long Time Coming

Alberta is the second last province to grant Treaty Indians the right to vote in provincial elections, in 1965. Only Québec takes longer.

Two Strikes and You're Not Even Out

William Hawrelak is the Edmontonian with the distinction of being the only mayor forced to resign his office *twice* over dodgy land deals—once in 1959 and again in 1963 as he serves his fifth term as mayor. The voters don't seem to care because in 1974 he wins a sixth term as mayor by a landslide 49 percent of the vote.

The Queen's Historian

In 1965, Grant MacEwan, author, historian and former Calgary mayor, becomes Alberta's ninth lieutenant-governor.

All the Way to the Top

The first governor general of Canada to be born in Alberta is Roland Michener, appointed in 1967.

Youngest Chief

The youngest-ever president of the Indian Association of Alberta is Harold Cardinal, elected when he is only 23, in 1968.

DID YOU  KNOW?

Peter Lougheed, who serves as Alberta premier from 1971 to 1985, played football for the Edmonton Eskimos.

Back and Forth, Then as Now

Once in power, Lougheed spends much of his time as premier battling it out with Ottawa and Pierre Trudeau over the National Energy Program. Albertans dislike the NEP because they judge it not only as an intrusion of federal government in an attempt to control the province's natural resources, but also a way of keeping prices lower than the market rate in order to benefit Easterners.

Out On a Limb

Some Albertans are so angry at the National Energy Program that a popular car sticker at the time reads: "Let the eastern b*st**ds freeze in the dark."

Disaster Dollars

In 1974, Alberta becomes Canada's third province to provide international aid in the face of natural and humanitarian disasters. By 1978 private and government donations from the province are larger than anywhere else in the country.

Royal Seal of Approval

Alberta's first Native lieutenant-governor is Saddle Lake Cree Ralph Steinhauer, appointed in 1974.

Chief Protest

The biggest First Nations demonstration ever in Alberta takes place in 1982, when over 5000 people gather on the steps of the Legislature to protest the Lougheed government's attempts to keep aboriginal and treaty rights out of the new Bill of Rights. The government loses the fight, and eventually the rights are affirmed.

Bloc Albertois!

The province's separatist leanings reach a peak when Gordon Kessler, a candidate for the Western Canada Concept Party, wins an MLA's seat in the Olds-Didsbury 1982 by-election. The party's manifesto includes independence for Alberta.

Never Really Takes Off

Although some polls claim there may be 40 percent of the Alberta population who support some form of independence from Ottawa, in the 2004 general election, the Separation Party of Alberta's 12 candidates win a mere 4680 votes, 0.5 percent of the provincial total.

Before His Time

Grant Notley, leader of Alberta's New Democratic Party, dies in an airplane crash in 1984. Notley began to lead the party when he was 29 and had been credited with turning the party into a viable political force during his 16 years as leader.

Mais Nous Sommes Bilingues!!!

In 1987, NDP's Leo Piquette, MLA for Lac La Biche, rocks the Legislature when he asks a question in, *sacré bleu!*, French! The Speaker tries to bring him to order three times until it is discovered that Section 110 of the North-West Territories Act of 1905 allows both official languages to be used in the Legislative Assembly. The Conservative government fights back—the French language is only allowed today in the legislature if an MLA gives at least two hours' notice.

First Lady

The first woman to become mayor of Edmonton is Jan Reimer in 1989. Alberta's first female Mayor is elected in Bellevue, a municipality in the Crowsnest Pass, in 1957. Canada's first female mayor is Charlotte Whitton, elected mayor of Ottawa in 1951.

Democratic Vote

Albertan WWII veteran Stan Waters wins the first election for a Senate seat in Canada, in 1989. After an eight-month delay, Prime Minister Mulroney appointed him to the Senate.

Change the Nation

In 1987, Preston Manning, the son of former Alberta premier Ernest Manning, becomes the first leader of the new federal party the Reform Party, which he founds. Manning serves as a Member of Parliament from 1993 to 2001. In 1989, Albertan Deborah Gray becomes the first Reform Party member to sit in Ottawa.

From Humble Beginnings

Ralph Klein, the senior civic affairs reporter with CFCN television, gets his first political job as mayor of Calgary in 1980. Klein is elected leader of the Alberta Progressive Conservatives on December 5, 1992—the first time a one-member one-vote system is used in a provincial leadership race. Eleven days later, on December 14, 1992, Klein is officially recognized as premier of Alberta—a post he still holds in 2006, though he promises to retire in October 2006. A promise he has made before.

More than Enough in the Coffers

For the first time since the 1980 oil crash, Alberta has a budget surplus in 1998, amounting to $2.6 billion.

It Runs in the Family

Ernest C. Manning, born in 1908, dies in 1996. A member of the Social Credit party, he was Alberta's longest-serving premier from 1943 to 1968.

Women of the Crown

At the turn of the century, in 2001, the lieutenant-governors in seven Canadian provinces (British Columbia, Alberta, Saskatchewan, Ontario, Québec, New Brunswick and Nova Scotia) and the governor general of Canada are women.

Tough Justice

Canada's first female chief justice of the Supreme Court is Albertan Beverley McLachlin, who is sworn into office in 2000.

GETTING BETTER

Western Medicine

Alberta's first pharmacy is licensed in 1884 by a J.D. Higinbotham in Fort Macleod. Higinbotham is also the first president of the Alberta Pharmaceutical Society and held certificate number 1 in that society.

Live Long and Prosper

At the time of Alberta becoming a province in 1905, the average life expectancy is 53 years.

Two-Tier Medicine

In 1914, a bed in a public ward of the newly constructed 20-bed hospital in the village of Coronation costs $2 a day or $3 for a private room.

Foreign Flu

The 1918 outbreak of Spanish influenza is so virulent that masks are worn in public, and public meetings throughout Alberta are banned. Thirty-eight thousand Albertans catch the disease, and 4000 die.

Paralysis Prevention

On September 7, 1927, in an attempt to contain a massive polio epidemic, provincial Health Minister George Hoadley issues drastic quarantine measures throughout the province.

Un-natural Selection

The Alberta government passes the Sexual Sterilization Act in 1928, that allows a specially created Eugenics Board to order the sterilization of any person deemed to be mentally defective. Three thousand people are sterilized until the Act is abolished 50 years later in 1978.

Payback Time

Leilani Muir is awarded $750,000 by an Alberta judge on January 25, 1996, as compensation for being wrongly diagnosed as mentally disabled and sterilized by the province's Eugenics Board in 1959. In 1999, the Alberta government compensates a further 247 mentally handicapped kids who were forcibly sterilized, to the tune of $80 million.

DID YOU KNOW?

Alberta is Canada's only rat-free province. However a few do appear in the province from time to time. Public health officials are shocked to find a few of the vermin in their midst on July 19, 1950. They've been gotten rid of since.

Don't Forget to Floss

Alberta's first dental hygienist, Ms. Joan Engman, studies dental hygiene in Michigan and returns to Alberta to practise in 1951.

We Can See You

Alberta's first mobile x-ray clinic tours the province in 1945.

Canada's First Open-Heart Surgery

Dr. John Callaghan performs the first operation of its kind in Canada in 1956 at Edmonton's University of Alberta Hospital. Callaghan is also the co-inventor of the world's first cardiac pacemaker in 1950. He is awarded the Alberta Order of Excellence in 1986

Baby Bust

Although the Pill becomes available in 1961 and is prescribed by doctors to "regulate the menstrual cycle," it is only legalized as a birth control method in 1969. Two years later, the Calgary Birth Association is born. A rape crisis centre is created about the same time as part of the women's equality movement.

Looking into Livers

Canada's first organ transplant research group starts up on April 2, 1970, a joint project between the Medical Research Council and the University of Alberta.

New Heart for an Old Guy

Lloydminster's Nelson Lumber Company millionaire Ray Nelson becomes the oldest heart transplant patient in the world in 1999, at the age of 79.

Miracle Method

Using a new technique called the Edmonton Protocol in 2000, a University of Alberta medical team transplants human pancreatic cells into eight severely diabetic people, who successfully begin producing their own insulin. The procedure is hailed worldwide as an effective control of Type 1 diabetes, until 2005 when the transplanted cells show evidence of reduced effectiveness.

Smoking Kills

Edmontonian Barb Tarbox, dies on May 18, 2003. She is posthumously awarded the Meritorious Service Medal of Canada on December 5, 2003, seven months after her death, for her dedication to the anti-smoking cause. The award is made by Her Excellency, The Right Honourable Adrienne Clarkson, Governor General of Canada. When Barb discovers she has stage 4 cancer in 2002 as a result of smoking since she was 11, she spends the last few months of her life trying to convince young kids not to pick up the habit.

GROWING SUCCESS

King of the Crop

In 1909, Marquis wheat is distributed to farmers in the province for the first time. Ontario scientist Charles Saunders develops the strain in 1904 from a Ukrainian wheat seed and sends 400 samples to farmers throughout western Canada. Since then the wheat has dominated farming in Alberta and Saskatchewan because of the high quality of its grain and flour, its early ripening, resistance to low temperatures and high yield, and the fact that its straw does not lie flat.

Crop-munchers Poisoned
In 1922, villagers in Coronation baited a swarm of grasshoppers with 40 tonnes of grain impregnated with a tonne of arsenic.

Champ of Champions

Herman Trelle of Peace River country wins the World Wheat Growing Championships in 1926.

Cream of the Crop
In 1933, Ralph Bailey sets up a creamery, 10 kilometres south of Cold Lake. The site evolves into the town of Grand Centre, which is selected as the end of a branch line of the CPR. Grand Centre is incorporated as a town in 1958.

Covering the Essentials
Farmers in the Depression are paid to stay on their farms and given $5 a month to cover basic food necessities. Prices are 60 cents for 10 pounds of sugar, 40 cents per pound for coffee, 30 cents per yard for cloth, 5 gallons of cream for $1.98 and 1.5 cents per pound for beef. The provincial government also buys cattle for 2 cents per pound. (One pound is equivalent to 0.453 kilograms; one gallon equals 4.5 litres; one yard equals .9 metres.)

CATTLE AND CONFECTIONERY

Finish a Cow, Then Finish It Off

The term "to finish" a cow means to fatten it up before slaughter. The first commercial feedlot in Alberta starts in 1928. It finishes 3000 head of cattle with by-products from the next-door sugar-beet farm.

Growing Industry

In the 1938–39 winter feeding season, six companies feed cattle in operations so successful that the number of feeders triples within four years. Cattlemen are no longer dependent on just hay to feed their stock. By 1961, 116 feedlot operators are pumping cattle with grains and cattle feed as well as hay.

Good Breeding

By 1945, 80 percent of Alberta's cattle are Herefords.

Soaking the Fields

Alberta is one of the world's leaders in irrigation technology. Canada's first central pivot sprinkler system (a long revolving arm laden with sprinklers), is erected on a farm near Bow Island in 1961. Also in Bow Island, a completely automated water distribution system is installed in 1982, by the St. Mary's River Irrigation District, serving an area of 20 km².

Wonderfully Waterlogged

By 1960, Alberta boasts about 243,000 hectares of irrigated land. By 1973, 405,000 hectares are irrigated out of a total of 20.5 million hectares of agricultural land.

Get Off My Back, Sunny

Desperate to grow a crop free of government regulation, Tom Droog decides to grow sunflower seeds. The first crop in 1979 sells primarily as birdseed but the following year Droog roasts the seeds, packages them into one-pound bags (about half a kilogram), and the brand name Spitz, beloved by campers and blue-collar workers, is born.

The World's Largest Milkshake

The creamy concoction is cooked up in Edmontonians on July 24, 1988. They use 20,000 kilograms of ice cream, 4400 kilograms of syrup and 240 kilograms of topping to make a thirst-quencher that weighs about 25,000 kilograms.

Milking It

Edmonton Oilers' owner Peter Pocklington sells Palm Dairies to Beatrice Foods of Toronto for an estimated $100 million on July 19, 1990.

Danger in the Food Chain

A cow already made into dog food is found to have had Mad Cow Disease (bovine spongiform encephalopathy) on May 20, 2003, on a northern Alberta farm. The U.S. and 34 other countries close their borders to Canadian beef, causing massive problems for the $7.6 billion beef industry. In July 2005, the U.S. reopens its borders for cattle under 30 months old.

Never Too Late for a Great Idea

Jean Paré is 53 years old when she self-publishes her first cookbook in 1981 out of a basement office in Vermilion. She designed *150 Delicious Squares* to put right all the things she hated about cookbooks at the time. She comes up with a winning formula: a single subject, lay-flat book binding, full-colour photos, and simple tried-and-tested recipes made from ingredients most people have in their kitchens. Unaware that a bestseller moves around 5000 copies, she prints 15,000 of her first edition and sells out within three months. Today Paré presides over the *Company's Coming* publishing empire, which releases 10 new titles worth $10 million a year.

What Would Albertans Do Without Him?

Many Albertans thank the lord Bernard Callebaut falls in love with the Rockies and decides to move to Calgary from Belgium. He brings with him recipes for gourmet handmade chocolates and inaugurates his first Calgary store to sell luxurious confectionery on March 23, 1983. Today there are 35 locations province-wide where chocaholics can lick their lips.

Processing Food

By 2002, the province's largest manufacturing sector is the food and beverage processing industry. The industry accounts for a quarter of the province's manufacturing sector or $9.8 billion of total manufactured goods in 2002, which is more than the province's earnings from petrochemical manufacturing (an average of $9 billion). In Canada, Alberta is the third largest producer of food and beverages.

EARLY SUCCESS

A Fortune Won and Lost

John Walter is Edmonton's first millionaire. He arrives from the Orkney Isles, Scotland, at Fort Edmonton in 1870 and runs a successful boat building and ferry business. He opens a sawmill in 1893, paying his labourers $1.75 per day. Next he opens a coal mine which pays $4 per day. But then his empire collapses in a series of calamities. The final blow, the North Saskatchewan River flood of 1915, destroys his lumber mill.

Canadian Loyalist

He arrives in a boxcar in 1910 along with 2000 other black farmers and entrepreneurs from the U.S. The first winter brings temperatures of -50°C. But Jeff Edwards prospers into a successful farmer and community leader, the man behind Amber Valley's infrastructure and coach of the region's famous baseball team.

A Novel Businesswoman

Evelyn De Mille, a former shop assistant in Eaton's book department, buys her first Calgary bookstore in 1956 with $1200 and goes on to become the first woman in Canada to own a chain of them called Evelyn De Mille Books.

EXCEPTIONAL ALBERTANS

A Model of a Village…

German émigré Martin Nordegg finds two massive seams of coal in the Rockies in 1911, which he develops into Canada's largest mine. His dream is to build a model village for the workers and their families, rather than have them live in the dreadful conditions existing in other mining towns. By 1915, he builds a town filled with rows of pastel-coloured houses and churches, a hotel, theatre, the huge Big Horn Trading Company store and a 19-bed hospital, considered the most modern in central Alberta.

…But No Fairytale Ending

But when WWI breaks out, Nordegg was declared by the Canadian government to be an "enemy alien." All German ownership of the town and the mine are obliterated. Martin Nordegg is removed from his positions of authority, and his dreams destroyed. Despite what is marked on today's highway signs and maps, the town's name was officially changed to Brazeau.

Meat King of Western Canada

On the back of a successful chain of butchers shops, Pat Burns builds up his company into one of the world's largest meat-packing and food distribution businesses, with 7 packing plants, 100 butchers, 65 creamery and cheese factories and 29 wholesale supply warehouses. Burns celebrates his 75th birthday in 1931 with 700 guests tucking into a 2-tonne birthday cake. His estate on his death at 81 in 1937 is valued at $3.8 million.

The Love Bug

Lois Elsa Hole is known as Alberta's most colourful characters. Called the "Queen of Hugs" for breaking protocol and hugging everyone she meets, whether they be other politicians, journalists, diplomats or ordinary folk. Lois excels as a businesswoman of a successful market garden company, the author of bestselling books, an educator, politician and the 15th lieutenant-governor of Alberta from February 10, 2000, until her death on January 6, 2005.

DID YOU  KNOW?

Lois Hole was only one member of a remarkable family. All of her seven brothers and her sister were graduates of the University of Alberta. The Holes are Alberta's most successful dynasty with interests in industrial, petrochemical, water treatment and mining-related construction held by the company Lockerbie and Hole.

429 Days Around the World

Ben Gray, a retired bison rancher, captains a shallow-draft yacht called Idlewild on a 50,000-kilometre circumnavigation of the globe starting on May 24, 2005. He casts off at the Dunvegan Bridge in Peace River Country. Also aboard are his sons Kevin and Brad. The crew cruise down the Peace, Slave and Mackenzie Rivers, reach the Arctic Ocean and take the Northwest Passage to the Atlantic Ocean and the rest of the world. They arrive back in Prince Rupert on July 27, 2006. Ben was born in Brooks and moved to Silver Valley, northern Alberta in 1989 to run the Idlewild Bison Ranch.

Sewing Up the Province

Charles A. Graham is the founder of Edmonton's Great Western Garment Co. (GWG) in 1910. He put the company's success down to being the first unionized manufacturing company in the province and the first to run on an eight-hour day. The Levi Strauss Co. buys GWG in 1911, and it becomes the largest producer of textiles in Western Canada due to a WWII contract for army uniforms. Ironically, the company closes in 2004 under pressure of cheaper imports from non-unionized nations.

Alberta's Howard Hughes

A compulsive recluse, Fred Charles Mannix (1914–91) hires PR people on condition they keep his name out of the papers or he docks their pay. Mannix builds a Calgary company of the same name into a billion-dollar business involved in construction, energy, real estate and broadcasting. When his former company secretary, Peter Lougheed, becomes premier in 1971, Mannix walks into his office and lays a piece of paper on his desk declaring: "This is your cabinet." Not one of the names made it.

High-Class Builders

Ernest Poole's Poole Construction Company makes it through the Depression by crunching gravel for roads. Poole moves his corporate HQ from Saskatchewan to Edmonton in 1932 and goes from strength to strength. After a fire, the company rebuilds the Jasper Park Lodge in under a year. It's the sort of project management that turns PCL into the biggest general construction contracting company in Canada and one of the largest in the U.S., with an annual turnover of $3.1 billion.

Queen of the Skies

Lethbridge-born Rosella Bjornson starts flying lessons at 17 and goes on, in 1973, to become the first female airline pilot and first officer in North America to fly a jet, a Fokker-28 65-seat passenger jet for Transair. She swaps places in the cockpit in 1990 and takes up the right-hand seat when she became Canada's first female captain, flying a Boeing 737.

Backbreaking Pioneers

After literally breaking his back in the Yukon mines and spending a year in traction, Frank Spinelli opens Edmonton's Italian Centre Shop in 1961 with the motto "Enjoy today. Pay when you can." His generosity earns him a thriving business with loyal clientele, a park named in his honour and a bronze statue depicting him playing cards with his cronies.

NATURAL HISTORY

Canada's Mini Grand Canyon

Seventy million years of history are carved into the rock at Horseshoe Canyon (17 kilometres southwest of Drumheller), creating spectacular badlands formations.

A Freezing Province

Alberta, along with the rest of Canada, suffers an ice age about 10,000 years ago.

The Greatest Story Ever Told

The acoustically superb 2500-seat natural bowl amphitheatre in the Badlands of central Alberta creates the perfect stage to go back 2000 years for an annual Passion play, depicting the life, death and resurrection of Jesus Christ. It is listed as "Alberta's Top Cultural Attraction" by *Attractions Canada* and one of the "Top 100 Events in North America" by the American Bus Association.

A Silver Lining

In 1886, Philip Stanley Abbot, a wealthy Boston lawyer, falls 300 metres to his death in an attempt to climb Mount Lefroy (on the border of Banff and Yoho Park). Amid cries to ban mountaineering, his father and friends do the opposite. They honour Abbot by "conquering" the mountain's peak the following year. The CPR realizes this is the beginning of a trend and hires two Swiss guides to make the mountains safer. A new era in outdoor recreation is born.

DID YOU KNOW?

The word "Yoho," as in Yoho National Park, is the Cree word for "wow."

Ice Age
The lowest temperature ever recorded in Alberta is –61°C, on January 11, 1911, at Fort Vermilion, Alberta.

That's Got a Ring to It

Sounding Lake, nestled in the Neutral Hills (27 kilometres north of Consort), is so called after an Indian legend. In the legend, the Great Eagle, *Mikisew*, emerges from the waters with its enormous wings roaring like thunder as it takes off across these hills.

Neither For Nor Against

The Neutral Hills are so called to commemorate the place where the Blackfoot and the Cree declare a truce after fighting over bison in the area for decades. They realize sharing the bounty is more beneficial than fighting over it.

Seasonal Crossing
Until 1911, the only overland route to the Peace River is from Edmonton to Lesser Slave Lake, then across country to Dunvegan. It is only passable in winter when the rivers, muskeg (swamps) and lakes are frozen. Mirror Landing, near present-day Smith, located on the shores of Lesser Slave Lake at the mouth of the Athabasca, is a bustling town and supply base used by the railroad builders. But once the train track is complete, the town falls into ruin.

Fireproof Bricks

City officials in Calgary promote the use of sandstone as a building material after a massive fire in 1912 sweeps through the city, which is soon nicknamed the "sandstone city."

Candy Floss and Ice-Cream Sold Here
Since 1901, Sylvan Lake has been a summer mecca for land-locked beach lovers. The only operational lighthouse between Winnipeg and the West Coast is built here in 1988 to celebrate the lake's 75th anniversary.

Weird Wiggling Wormies

Edmonton experienced a freak dump of heavy rain on August 9, 1913. It results in large numbers of earthworms wriggling their way through mud onto city streets.

Water Water Everywhere

The Bassano Dam on the Bow River opens on April 25, 1914, designed to hydrate the Eastern Irrigation District, an area of over 600,000 hectares. The dam is 107 metres wide at its base and built of earth.

River Runs Through It

On June 28, 1915, the North Saskatchewan River in Edmonton rises three metres in 10 hours. A day later it is 14.5 metres above normal levels and floods the riverflat communities of the city.

A Place to Yodel

Swiss guides brought to Banff by the Canadian Pacific Railway build an alpine-style stone hut in 1923 called the Abbott Pass Refuge Cabin. The lodge serves as a high altitude base for generations of climbers and is designated a National Historic Site in 1992.

More Tea, Vicar?

Mrs. Gertrude Crosy, originally from England realizes there is nowhere to go for afternoon tea around the increasingly popular tourist resort of Lake Louise. So she builds Red Deer Lodge, a log teahouse, in 1923. The place turns into the must-visit place for crumpets and Early Grey, as well as an hotel which, compared to the nearby Chateau Lake Louise, offers moderately priced accommodation. The original cabin is now the hotel's dining room.

Whirlwind Province

Forty tornadoes rip up central
Alberta on July 7 and 8, 1927.
Three people are killed near
Wetaskiwin, and Rocky Mountain
House is shredded.

A Stunning Site

The Prince of Wales Hotel, built
to look like a Swiss chateau, opens in 1927 in Waterton. It sits
on a location that is not only the showiest—a hill overlooking
the lake—but also the windiest. The chateau is rumoured to
have shifted 15 centimetres off its foundations since it was built.
Today the hotel is a designated National Historic Site.

Worth the Effort

Reached only by an 11-kilometre trek from Lake Louise, the
Skoki Lodge in Banff National Park becomes Canada's first
commercial backcountry holiday facility in 1931. It is built by
a group of ski enthusiasts and still operates today.

Peace and Quiet

In 1932, the Rotary Clubs of Alberta and Montana unite their
two parks into the world's first international peace park, the
Waterton Glacier International Peace Park. Named by
UNESCO as a World Heritage Site in 1995, the organization
describes it as being "exceptionally rich in plant and mammal
species as well as prairie, forest and alpine and glacial features."

Sacred Symbol

Iron Creek, near the modern town of Sedgwick, gets its name
from the large chunks of iron-impregnated rock found nearby.

Landing Pad

Iron Creek is also the place that Canada's largest meteorite, the Manitou Stone weighing around 150 kilograms, falls to earth. But the stone arrives so long ago the exact date is now unknown. The Indians revere the stone and leave sacrifices there.

Manitou Moved
The stone is spotted by Alexander Henry in September 1810 and moved by John McDougall in 1869 to the Victoria College Museum in Toronto. The following year a smallpox epidemic decimates the Cree and the bison herds across the province—First Nations people believe it is a result of bad medicine caused by the stone's removal. The stone is returned to the province and is now housed in the Royal Alberta Museum, Edmonton.

A Blast of Hot Air

On January 7, 1932, a Calgary Chinook (warm wind from the Pacific Ocean) causes a 29-degree swing in temperature from –22°C to 7°C.

Landlocked Beach Park
Alberta gets its first provincial park at Aspen Beach, on November 21, 1932. The park is located on the banks of Gull Lake, 17 kilometres west of Lacombe on Highway 12.

Slippery Slope

The 300-kilometre-long Icefields Parkway opens in 1940, connecting Banff and Jasper. It becomes known as one of the most scenic routes in the world.

A Massive Dump

Fifty centimetres of snow falls on Edmonton on November 15, 1942.

The Best Dino Graveyard in the World

Dinosaur Provincial Park is created in 1955 in a region of badlands and coulees that seem to show outer space merging with the desert. The park is named a UNESCO World Heritage Site in 1979 and contains some of the most important fossil discoveries ever made from the Age of Reptiles—in particular, 35 species of dinosaurs dating back 75 million years. The area is found along the Red Deer River in southeastern Alberta near the town of Brooks.

Ripping up Rooftops

Calgary and vicinity sustains $100 million dollars worth of damage during a 15-minute hailstorm on July 28, 1981.

National Treasure

The Cave and Basin Hot Springs are discovered by three railway workers in 1883, leading to the creation of Banff National Park, Canada's first. Fittingly, the springs themselves are declared a National Historic Site in 1981.

Universal Treasure

The site of a laboratory built at the top of Sulphur Mountain, Banff, to study cosmic rays during the International Geophysical Year (1957–58), is designated a National Historic Site in 1982.

Royal Old Bones

The Tyrrell Museum of Paleontology in Drumheller opens to the public on September 25, 1985. It is renamed the Royal Tyrrell Museum in 2005 after a visit from Queen Elizabeth II.

Winds of Wrath

The worst tornado to hit Alberta strikes Edmonton on July 31, 1987. The twister stays on the ground for over an hour, damaging $330 million worth of property, injuring hundreds, killing 27 people and destroying 300 homes.

Hailstorm Alley

Alberta has some of the worst hailstorms in the world. Calgary holds the record for a massive dump on September 7, 1991, when ice as big as baseballs smashes property to the tune of $237 million, not including $105 million worth of insurance claims for battered cars.

Jump in the Lake

The Oldman River Dam project is completed in 1991 in response to droughts on southern Alberta farms, despite protests by environmentalists and First Nations. The Dam is located where the Oldman, Castle and Crowsnest Rivers meet. Interestingly, irrigated lands in Alberta account for 12 percent of the agricultural output even though irrigated lands are only 5 percent of the total farmed land in Alberta.

Leftovers from an Ancient Lunch

Digging an oil pipeline in 1995 south of Provost, workers uncover a bison kill with skeletons and bones dating back 5000 years. University of Alberta researchers are called in to conduct an archeological dig and research in the newly created Bodo Archeological Site.

Shopping Washout

The biggest rainstorm in Edmonton history on July 11, 2004, causes more than $100 million in damage. West Edmonton Mall is evacuated, and roads, houses and businesses flood.

Sign o' the Times
Because of the U.S. embargo on softwood from Canada, a major player in the industry, Cowley Forest Products/Johnson Bros. located near the Crowsnest Pass, closes its doors in November 2002.

FIRSTS AND LASTS

Pit Stop

The first "store" in Alberta is built by fur trader Peter Pond who opens a trading post near Lake Athabasca in 1778.

Full Steam Ahead

The first river steamer, the *Northcote,* arrives in Edmonton on July 22, 1875.

Mail Man

Edmonton's first post office opens on March 1, 1878.

Start the Press

Alberta's first newspaper, the *Edmonton Bulletin*, begins publication on December 8, 1880. Two years later Fort Macleod gets its own paper, the *Fort Macleod Gazette.*

Another Messenger

The Calgary Herald, Mining and Ranch Advocate and General Advertiser starts life in a tent on the banks of the Elbow River on August 31, 1883. A tiny printing press spits out the four pages of the paper's first run.

Telecommunications Take Hold

The Canadian Government telegraph from Selkirk, Manitoba to Hay Lakes near Edmonton is completed in 1876. The first service to Calgary spells its first dot-dot-dashes in 1877. The first person in Calgary to receive a message is James Walker, a member of the North-West Mounted Police.

Do as You're Told
The telegraph line almost doesn't make it to Hay Lakes, because the man in charge of building it, Alex Taylor, discovers there's no one actually living there. So, in his wisdom, Taylor writes the government in Ottawa suggesting he end the line in Edmonton instead. The reply reads: "A pox upon you for your impertinence. That god-like individual, the Honourable Minister of the Interior, has directed that there is a settlement at Hay Lakes. Therefore, you will open a telegraph office there, as directed." Taylor does as he is told but has extra cable so extends the telegraph to Edmonton anyway.

Tree Slicers
Canmore becomes home to western Canada's first sawmill in 1881.

Hello! Is Anyone There?
Alexander Taylor, a Dominion telegraph agent in Edmonton, sets up Alberta's first telephone link in 1884 with two phones he's ordered from England. The first call made on the system is from the one phone in Edmonton to the other in St. Albert.

Town Building
Calgary is incorporated as a town in 1884 and in 1885 builds its first town hall and jail out of wood at a total cost of $1694.

First Traffic Accident
Two carts smash into each other on April 27, 1893, on the corner of Jasper Avenue and 101 Street, Edmonton, injuring three men.

The Lights Go On
Calgary is the first town in the province to get hooked up with electricity in 1887.

A Long Day Trip
A place in 1906 history is reserved for Mr. H. White who makes the first road trip from Edmonton to Calgary by car in a 12-hour drive.

Not So Fast

The speed limit in 1905 is 10 miles per hour (16 kilometres per hour) in town, 20 miles per hour (32 kilometres per hour) in the country.

Premier Rutherford's Baby

Under the new premier's direction, the City of Edmonton buys the Edmonton and District Telephone Company and creates North America's first municipally owned phone company in 1905. It is called City Telephones, a brand that endures for 66 years. In 1908, the company installs automatic dialing, again the first in North America.

Safe and Sound

The prize for becoming Canada's first wildlife sanctuary for large animals goes to Elk Island National Park (east of Edmonton), founded in 1906.

A Wonderful Link

The first streetcar from Edmonton to Strathcona crosses the Low Level Bridge on October 31, 1908.

Fighting Over Lessons

The University of Alberta holds its first class in 1908 in Edmonton. When rival city Calgary wants to set up a university of its own in 1912, the provincial government refuses on the grounds the province cannot sustain two universities.

On a Wing and a Prayer

Alberta's first aeroplane flight takes off in 1911.

A Love of Flying

Recently-returned aviators from WWI start up their own air companies. Blatchford Field, Air Harbour No. 1, is established at this time, and now is known as Edmonton's City Centre Airport. In 1918, Katherine Stinson flies the first airmail trip in Canada, from Calgary to Edmonton, in a Curtiss Special. By 1930, more air cargo and mail is flown from Alberta than anywhere else in the country

Mazeltov to Builders
Work starts on Edmonton's first Jewish synagogue in 1911.

A Fistful of Firsts

The man behind Edmonton's first ambulance service, first airport and first bus route between Edmonton and St. Albert is John McNeil who gets his empire up and running in 1911.

Book Lender

Alberta's first public library is opened in Calgary in 1912.

Time to Get Off

Alberta's last train robbery is the work of three miners, George Arkoff, Ausby Auloff and Tom Bassoff. They successfully rob Canadian Pacific Railway train No. 63 at the Crowsnest Pass village of Bellevue on August 20, 1920.

Saved on Celluloid

Buffalo National Park is set up in Wainwright in 1913 to save one of the province's last remaining herds of bison. The park is the location, in October 1923, of Alberta's first Hollywood movie. *The Last Frontier* features a bison stampede amid untouched prairie as far as the eyes can see. One hundred Natives from Hobbema act as extras.

Making the World Smaller

George Rice delivers Edmonton's first radio broadcast on May 1, 1922, at the CJCA radio station transmitting from the roof of the *Edmonton Journal*. With the technology so new, few individuals had their own sets, so radio programming is received by radios in auditoriums where groups gather. Later, Rice sets up *Sunwapta Broadcasting*, mother of today's CFRN Television.

Growing Old Gracefully

Alberta's first "Old Age Pension" cheque is issued on August 31, 1929, partly subsidized by the federal government.

Don't Go on Red

The first traffic light in Edmonton is hung on the corner of Jasper Avenue and 101 Street in 1932.

Make Way for Modernization

The last streetcar in Calgary makes its last run on December 29, 1950.

No More Visits

The last great caribou migration passes by Fort Chipewyan in 1951.

Planes on the Plains

Edmonton International Airport's first plane takes off in 1960.

Milking It

In 1961, the last horse-drawn milk carriage in Edmonton gives up the reins.

As Tough as They Get
The first female combat soldier in Canada, Heather Erxleben, graduates from Canadian Forces Base Wainwright on January 19, 1989.

Tough in the Air Too
Jane Foster and Deanna Brasseur pass the course at Cold Lake to become Canada's, if not the world's, first female fighter pilots available for combat roles. The date is June 9, 1989.

On the Edge of Extinction

During the 1800s, the whooping crane, with its distinctive bugle-like cry, is plentiful and numbers around 1500. But the bird's numbers drop after it becomes a fashionable trophy in Victorian drawing rooms, and its wetland homes are drained by farmers. It becomes one of the most threatened species in the world and is found today only in nesting grounds within Wood Buffalo National Park.

Hiding Place Spotted

By the 1940s, only 16 cranes remain. In 1954, a helicopter pilot spots a couple of birds, which mate for life, with a chick. This leads to the discovery of the birds' near-mythical hideout, and since then conservation efforts have brought the whooping crane population up to between 185 and 300.

HIGHS AND LOWS

Holy to Many

Manito Sakahigan (Spirit Lake), located 60 kilometres east of Edmonton, is revered for centuries by First Nations as a spot for ceremonial gatherings around the buffalo hunt. In 1844, Father Jean-Baptiste Thibault blesses the lake and renames it in honour of St. Anne, the mother of the Virgin Mary.

A Healing Trip

In 1889, 400 people attend a pilgrimage to Lac Ste. Anne, and since then, the annual pilgrimage numbers have grown to 40,000, turning the annual event into the largest of its kind in North America.

Way Up There

The town of Airdrie, which translates as the "King's Heights," is appropriately named in 1889. When Airdrie became Alberta's 15th city in 1985, it also became the city with the highest elevation in Canada, at 978 metres above sea level.

Anything that Moves

Wetaskiwin is also home to one of Alberta's 18 provincially owned and operated historic sites and museums, the Reynolds-Alberta Museum. The place is a shrine to one of the world's best collections of machines, and to the history of mechanization in industry, aviation, agriculture and transport in the province from the 1890s to the 1970s. More than 3500 vehicles, 70 airplanes and 1000 pieces of agricultural equipment are on display.

Truly Cheap

"Cars Cost Less in Wetaskiwin." After the City's car dealers collaborate on a single marketing and advertising campaign in the 1990s, more cars are sold here than anywhere else in Canada.

TIMETABLES OF TOWNS AND CITIES

LOCATION	INCORPORATION AS A TOWN	INCORPORATION AS A CITY
Calgary	1884	1894
Edmonton	1892	1904
Lethbridge	1890	1906
Medicine Hat	1898	1906
Wetaskiwin	1902	1906
Strathcona	1899	1907
Red Deer	1901	1913
Camrose	1906	1955
Grande Prairie	1919	1958
Lloydminster	1903	1958
St. Albert	1861	1977
Fort McMurray	1947	1980
Leduc	1906	1983
Fort Saskatchewan	1904	1985
Airdrie	1974	1985
Banff	1880	1990
Spruce Grove	1971	1996
Cold Lake	1996	2000
Jasper	1913	2001
Brooks	1910	2005

The Best of the Well-Dressed

Starting from humble beginnings on Edmonton's 102nd Street, La Fleche Bros. becomes the tailor of choice to the rich and famous worldwide from the 1920s onwards. The fourth-generation descendants of founding brothers Joseph and Tripoli run the store today.

Fashionable to Recycle

In the first decade of the 1900s, white velvet wedding dresses are at the height of fashion. This luxury item is so expensive it is later often used to line coffins for unfortunate members of the same family.

British Roots

Many towns in Alberta take their names from British settlements: Banff, Carstairs, Edmonton, Didsbury, Airdrie and Mallaig.

Fit for a King

In June 1911, the town of Coronation, in the heart of the arid Palliser's Triangle in southeastern Alberta, is named the year after George V's Coronation. The same year, the town's theatre, the Star, is delivered on runners trundled through the snow! The theatre remains a focal point for entertainment for the next 40 years.

Alberta's Oldest Barbershop and Pool Hall

The Pool Hall is built on the town of Vilna's Main Street in 1921. Today the Hall still displays the original tables including two 4-metre Brunswick Balke Collender snooker tables and two 2.5-metre Samuel May billiard tables. Also on display are the original cues, balls, racks, Booker coal heater, benches, counters, advertisements, oiled wood floors and barber's chair. The Hall is now a provincially designated registered historic resource.

Phew, What a Scorcher

Alberta's hottest temperature ever recorded is 43.3°C in Brooks, in July 1931. A decade later, the same high is recorded in Fort Macleod.

Breeding Gone Barking Mad

A rabbit infestation in Drayton Valley is so bad in the 1920s that anyone chopping down a tree sees it stripped bare of bark by morning.

From Moo to Zoo

It's not just cows that thrive in Alberta. The Calgary Zoo first opens in 1929 and is Canada's second largest today.

Eastern European Fungus

Vilna, 55 kilometres northeast of Edmonton, is said to be named for Wilno, a large city in Poland, by émigrés from that city who settled the town. The town's other claim to fame is being the site of the world's largest mushroom—a metal sculpture.

City Drought

Even in 1949, most Edmontonians had no running water so it was trucked in at a cost of $1.25 for 500 gallons (about 2300 litres).

Fly the French Flag

Alberta has a Franco-Albertan flag, designed by Jean Pierre Grenier for a competition organized by the French Youth Association of Alberta in 1982. The flag features two triangles: a blue one to represent the population of Alberta and a white one within it, to represent the French-speaking population. Two flowers are also featured: the wild rose (the official emblem of Alberta) and the fleur-de-lys (the symbol of the French-speaking world).

Shrinking Among the Giants

In 1910, the tallest building in Calgary is the six-storey Grain Exchange Building. The Palliser Hotel, 12 storeys high, is the tallest until 1958. The Calgary Tower is built in 1968 to commemorate Canada's Centennial, by architect Bill Milne, at a cost of $3.5 million. When completed, it is the city's tallest building at 190 metres.

Modern Giants

Today the tallest building in Calgary is the Petro-Canada building at 215 metres (53 storeys), completed in 1984. The 1989 East and West Banker's Halls are 196.5 metres (52 storeys) high. Today a new skyscraper is being built, the Encana New Building Project, planned at 60 storeys or 350 metres high.

His Holiness Comes Calling

Pope John Paul II visits Alberta in September 1984. The spot at Elk Island National Park where he sat to contemplate is commemorated with a bench. The Edmonton hillside where His Holiness spoke to well-wishers (the same hillside that hosts the annual Edmonton FolkFest) is marked with a metal sculpture called the Dove of Peace.

Retail Therapy

Construction begins on Phase 1 of West Edmonton Mall in 1981. The shopping centre remains the biggest in the world until overtaken in size by the Golden Resources Mall in Beijing in 2004, which has 14 percent more floor space.

Ride of Doom
Three people die at West Edmonton Mall when its Schwarzkopf "Mindbender" roller coaster derails on June 14, 1986.

Bombs Away
On February 20, 1985, a missile is released from a B-52 bomber over the Beaufort Sea in the Arctic. It makes its way to its target, Primrose Lake, Alberta, thereby accomplishing the first successful U.S. cruise missile test in Canadian airspace.

Pampering Profitability

In 2003, Eveline Charles becomes the first woman inducted into the Alberta Business Hall of Fame, Junior Achievement. Charles has made a fortune out of a company of the same name by stamping her initials, EC, on everything from soaps and lipsticks to light fittings. Branding is the secret of the success of her day spas, founded in 1984, "one of the best and biggest personal care destinations in Canada." She was born in Falher, the honeybee capital of Alberta.

Tragic Trains
A head-on collision between a nine-car VIA Rail passenger train and a CN freight train at Hinton on February 8, 1986, leaves 29 people dead and 93 injured.

No Remorse

In 1987, the Principal Group of Companies collapses in disgrace. This Edmonton financial investment institution lost $427 million dollars, invested by 67,000 mostly elderly Canadians. Despite the collapse, the company's owner Donald Cormie remains a wealthy man worth millions. The scandal has been billed as the most shocking failure of a financial institution in Canadian history and a total failure of government and regulatory bodies to stop fraud.

Massive Mobile Home

On September 12, 1991, the world's largest tipi is erected at Medicine Hat. Known as the Saamis Tipi, it is originally used as a symbol of the 1988 Calgary Olympics.

Coming of Age

In 1992, the Siksika tribe, once part of the powerful Blackfoot Confederacy, register their nation's symbol as a coat of arms with the Canadian Heraldic Authority—volume one, number one, in the First Nations category.

More Love Bugs and Bears

A year to the day after the September 11, 2001, terrorist attacks in New York and Washington, seven-year-old Lacey Brockhoff and four-year-old Haley Brockhoff, both of Edberg, Alberta, deliver nearly 2000 toy bears they have collected, with help from Edmonton's police department, to children who lost their parents that day. Alberta Premier Ralph Klein awards them a Great Kids award.

Provincial Singalong

Alberta has an official provincial song, called, erm, *Alberta*, adopted for the 2005 Centennial celebrations. Written by Mary Kieftenbeld, it is selected by a 13-member committee and recorded in both country and pop versions.

Truck Stop

Rimbey, 55 kilometres northwest of Red Deer, is home to the Smithson International Truck Museum, the world's largest collection of trucks.

Red River Raw Material

The town of Vermilion, in central Alberta, is famous for its early-1900s red bricks, made from riverbank clay, which can still be seen today on the façades of 28 historic downtown buildings.

STRANGE BUT TRUE

Look Behind You
The Banff Springs Hotel, which begins life in 1888, is believed to be home to a couple of ghosts—a bride who fell to her death continues to waltz around the grand ballroom and a doormen who is eager to "help" guests with their luggage.

An Evil Curse
In 1896, a man taking a stroll near Trout Lake, a creek located 104 kilometres northeast of Fort McMurray, reports seeing a strange creature. Over the next three days, the vision drives him mad and his body, according to witnesses, changes so much, it no longer resembles a human. Terrified, his fellow villagers believe the man is possessed by a windigo, a demonic spirit that eats humans. So, they execute him and pile logs on top of his grave to stop him getting out. The grave can still be seen, fenced off, near Trout Lake.

Free to Die
In 1924, the Edmonton Cemetery grants free burial plots to past members of the North West Mounted Police and members of the Canadian Legion.

Calgary's Gonners
Union Cemetery is Calgary's oldest grave-yard, established in 1891. But it is not the first. The Roman Catholic mission established St. Mary's Cemetery in 1876. This is the first final resting place, but the graves are later exhumed and moved to a new site on Macleod Trail.

The Great Wonders of the World

When electricity first is turned on at the Grand Hotel, in Okotoks, around 1910, a guest calls a maid to turn the light out because she can't blow it out.

Mystery Beast

Haunted Lake, just east of Alix near Buffalo Lake, is so called after a spooky incident, now recounted in legend. One winter night, the moon is shining brightly and the head of an elk is seen sticking out from the ice in the middle of the lake. Cree hunters, thinking the beast is dead, try to retrieve it, but as they approach, the elk moves off, the ice cracks and the hunters perish.

Red Means Stop

When officials from the City of Calgary meet with representatives from Canadian General Electric on April 23, 1928, to discuss the installation of electric traffic signs in the city, people at the meeting express concern that "drivers and pedestrians will dislike being regulated by a mechanical device."

Depressed Drivers

During the Great Depression of the 1930s, when gas for cars is unavailable or prohibitively expensive, automobiles are pulled by horses. The combinations are called "Bennett Buggies" after the Conservative prime minister.

Finger-Lickin' Critters

Colonel Sander's Kentucky Fried Chicken gravy recipe is developed in Bellevue, according to the town's website.

Disturbing or Delightful

The Gopher Hole Museum opens in 1996 after the town council decides to turn its gopher infestation into tourist dollars. The comical display of 54 stuffed gophers portrays 31 scenes of life in the town and is a must for anyone who ever wondered what a gopher would look like if it were dressed as a preacher. Or a lovelorn suitor. Or any one of a number of other anthropomorphic poses. International media descend on the town after People for the Ethical Treatment of Animals, PETA, protest. The museum has been the subject of controversy ever since and displays a book of hate mail from animal rights activists.

Politically Incorrect

A.W. Shackleford, mayor of Lethbridge, gets the fright of his life on February 14, 1953, when he picks up an improperly grounded microphone and receives a 50-volt shock for his trouble.

Is It a Bird? A Plane?

No, it's a meteor that lands near the hamlet of Abee, in central Alberta, in 1952. Weighing 107 kilograms, it is the heaviest visitor to the province from outer space recorded so far.

A Figment of Imagination
Len Mohr, a retired building contractor, starts construction on Em-Te Town in 1984. The "empty" town is an authentic-looking Western ghost town, located at Alder Flats, between Drayton Valley and Rocky Mountain House. The town features the Hogs Breath Saloon, a jailhouse, a harness shop, a livery stable, a bank, a church, and a restaurant. It's open all year round for visitors and used as a location for movies, as well as TV shows and commercials.

Is There Anyone Out There?

The world's only Unidentified Flying Object Landing-pad, measuring 12 metres across, is completed on June 3, 1967, and is ready to receive any wandering "mother ships." So far, the guest book is empty despite a 1976 CBC Radio report that a UFO entered Alberta airspace just before midnight on Christmas Eve. Could it have been Santa?

ABOUT THE AUTHOR

Marina Michaelides

Marina has always been so inquisitive about how the world works, she has never sat still. She was born a twin in London, England, to parents who emigrated there from the island of Cyprus. Marina received her degree in economics and management, and later a post-graduate diploma in communications. She worked as a documentary filmmaker in the UK for a decade, and in between projects, travelled all around the world searching for the meaning of life. Once she found out that it's all about loving the little things, she finally decided to settle down in Edmonton, Alberta. Marina continues to make award-winning documentaries for television, as well as write for magazines and journals…and she often loves to ponder the question of why we are here.

ABOUT THE
ILLUSTRATORS

Graham Johnson

Graham Johnson is an Edmonton-based illustrator and graphic designer. When he isn't drawing or designing, he...well...he's always drawing or designing! On the off-chance you catch him not doing one of those things, he's probably cooking, playing tennis or poring over other illustrations.

Roger Garcia

Roger Garcia immigrated to Canada from El Salvador at the age of seven. Because of the language barrier, he had to find a way to communicate with other kids. That's when he discovered the art of tracing. It wasn't long before he mastered this highly skilled technique, and by age 14, he was drawing weekly cartoons for the *Edmonton Examiner*. He taught himself to paint and sculpt; then in high school and college, Roger skipped class to hide in the art room all day in order to further explore his talent. Currently, Roger's work can be seen in a local weekly newspaper and in places around Edmonton.